T0331140

The Façade of Excellence

Defining a New Normal of Leadership

The Façade of Excellence
Defining a New Normal of Leadership

by
John Dyer

Routledge
Taylor & Francis Group

A PRODUCTIVITY PRESS BOOK

First edition published in 2020
by Routledge/Productivity Press
52 Vanderbilt Avenue, 11th Floor New York, NY 10017
2 Park Square, Milton Park, Abingdon, Oxon OX14 4RN, UK

International Standard Book Number-13: 978-0-367-14533-0 (Hardback)
International Standard Book Number-13: 978-0-429-03218-9 (eBook)

To my wife Keela

She has supported me in all of my endeavors and I love her dearly

To our children David, Danielle, and our son-in-law Kyle

Thank you for your love and encouragement and for
being the best family a Dad could hope for

And to all of the improvement professionals:

Keep working on transforming cultures, improving processes,
and applying the new normal of leadership in order to give
everyone the opportunity to be fulfilled and to experience
what it is like to be a part of a winning team

Contents

Acknowledgments

There are several people who have helped make this book possible who richly deserve recognition.

I thank my wife, Keela, who has proofread every article I have ever written and was the first person to read and provide feedback on each of the chapters in this book. Her perspective has been invaluable.

I appreciate and thank one of my previous bosses, Scott Duncan, who supported trying several of the ideas that are discussed in this book when he was the leader of a business. Over the years, Scott has also proofread everything I have written and has provided a business perspective, and for that I am eternally grateful.

Next, I extend many thanks to the person who gave me my first break in publishing, Jill Jusko, editor at *IndustryWeek* magazine. She has provided expert guidance and feedback throughout my writing career, and this book would not have been possible without her support.

Finally, I thank the folks at Productivity Press, Michael Sinocchi and Katherine Kadian, who have provided valuable insights into the publishing business and who were willing to take a chance on a little-known author.

John Dyer

Author

John Dyer has over 3 decades of Continuous Process Improvement experience: 10 years with General Electric, 10 years with Ingersoll-Rand (brand names included: Bobcat, Club Car, Schlage Lock, Thermo-King, and Hussmann), and the rest as President of John Dyer & Associates, Inc. – Process Innovations, a company that is focused on helping organizations of all types achieve excellence. He has a B.S. in Electrical Engineering from Tennessee Technological University and an M.S. in Business Management (International MBA) from Purdue University and the University of Rouen, France.

In the early 1990s while at GE, John was given a special assignment: go out and collect best practices in the area of Process Excellence. During this influential time in his career, he studied with Dr. Ed Deming, Brian Joiner (author of the Team Handbook), and attended classes at the Steven Covey Institute of Leadership and participated in the original Six Sigma training provided at Motorola University. From these best practices, John developed several interactive classes and workshops in the area of Continuous Improvement, including how to implement lean and Six Sigma, solve for the root cause of problems, and facilitate teams. After this assignment, the GE executives asked John to implement what he had learned. These experiences created the foundation for this book.

John is also a Contributing Editor for *IndustryWeek* magazine and a judge in the "IndustryWeek – Best Plant" competition (www.industryweek.com/author/john-dyer). He serves in several volunteer leadership positions in the United Methodist Church and enjoys spending time with friends and family.

Author John Dyer with Dr. W. Edwards Deming in 1991

Introduction

What are the characteristics of an outstanding leader? What does excellent leadership look like? Feel like? Sound like?

How much damage does an awful manager do to an organization? To the employees? To the customer relationship?

This book is for everyone ... current leaders and future leaders, those who are new in their career and those with several years of experience, people in manufacturing, the service industry, governments, hospitals, and non-profits. I believe that everyone will gain insight into the ways that managers and leaders are different and why it is important to the future success of your organization to fully understand these differences. My hope is that word will spread about the contents of this narrative and that the cultures of every organization will become a bit more focused on collaboration and teamwork. This is a dream I have had since my early days working at General Electric.

You will soon discover that this book is written in a style that is not the norm. Over the years, I have discovered that adults learn best when their imaginations are triggered. Throughout my time of writing articles for *IndustryWeek* magazine, I included a story based on real events followed by an analysis that would go into more depth on the key takeaways. When I was asked to turn some of these articles into a book, I decided to use this same style of writing. Each chapter begins with a narrative that involves two main characters: Frank Smith and Jim Brown. These two men are vice presidents in the fictional company known as JED, Inc. They both possess key characteristics of several people who I have worked for and with over the years. What occurs in the story portion of each chapter is based on actual events. Changes were made to protect the identity of the companies and people who were involved. Each chapter also contains an analysis of the narrative and provides practical applications.

The reader can choose to read the first portion of each chapter all of the way through the book and ignore the analysis. Some learn best this way. Others who want more of a business book can choose to ignore the story portions and just read the practical applications. Or, of course, one can read the book as written. I believe that all ways will work and be beneficial.

The story portion of the book is set within a manufacturing background. I picked this setting because that is what I know best and have the most experience. However, I do believe that anyone from any type of organization can learn the key lessons without this same set of experiences. For example, I am currently working with a group of police and firefighter leaders and walked them through several of the lessons outlined in this book. They were not only able to grasp the concepts but were also able to successfully apply the lessons to their own organizations. The same thing happened when I spoke to a group of government leaders. These lessons can benefit anyone who has a desire to help their organization move toward collaboration and teamwork in order to improve processes and culture.

Throughout this journey of discovering what it takes for an organization of any type to achieve excellence, I have been the most influenced by the teachings of Dr. W. Edwards Deming. Dr. Deming, a statistics professor, was asked by the U.S. government to go to Japan after World War II and lead an effort to perform a census. While there, Dr. Deming met with and educated many of the people who eventually became CEOs and leaders at various levels throughout Japanese corporations. He shared with these executives a different way to think about leading their organizations. They listened and implemented his teachings, resulting in the greatest revolution in quality, efficiency, innovation, and teamwork that the world has witnessed, in the private sector, in the past several decades. I was fortunate enough to participate in Dr. Deming's classes before his passing. One class, in 1991, was four days long, had about 750 participants, and was being broadcast via satellite to two other locations with approximately 750 observers. Dr. Deming conducted most of the four days entirely on his own. He was 90 years old. His passion for these topics was unmatched.

Dr. Deming spoke often about the need to eradicate fear, allow workers to build up pride in what they were doing, abolish the old management practices and substitute "leadership." Hopefully, this book will bring some of these teachings to life and help organizations of all types accelerate their own journey toward achieving excellence.

Thank you for reading this book. I hope it will inspire you to define a new normal of leadership in order to achieve excellence in all that you do.

John Dyer

1

Beginning the Road Toward Collaboration…

Perhaps everything we know about how to manage people is wrong

Two executives, Jim Brown and Frank Smith, are both vice presidents in the JED Company and oversee two similar divisions, each of which produces a product and provides several services. Jim Brown is new to the company and has a vision to transform the organizational culture in order to achieve excellence through the use of employee involvement, teamwork, and continuous improvement. This requires implementing a new style of leadership that lifts up the workers, encourages change, and promotes empowerment. Frank Smith utilizes the old ways of managing the workers through the use of control, goals, fear, and threats that creates a façade of excellence. This is their story...

THE STORY OF JIM BROWN

"I must be nocturnal," thought Officer Joe Brittain. He could not remember the last time he had slept when the sun was down. For the past 22 years, Joe had served as the night security guard for one of the JED, Inc. office complexes. He sat at his desk, working on a Sudoku puzzle when a beep from his phone reminded him that it was time to glance at a bank of security monitors that helped him see several areas of the building and parking lot. The sun had not yet crested the horizon, so many of the images were dark and difficult to decipher. He did not worry much about these difficulties since it had been quite some time since anything of importance had happened on his watch. The last issue he could remember occurred four years prior when a blaring alarm had gone off that was both deafening and irritating. It turned out that the screeching, ear-splitting alarm had been caused by a lonely rat running through the building, triggering one of the office security sensors.

"Hmmm…" thought Joe as he looked at the monitors. "Is that an old Ford pickup truck parked in the back of our employee lot? That is highly unusual since the office does not open for another hour." He zoomed in the camera image to get a better look and noticed a younger-looking man sitting behind the wheel. "He must have missed the 'No Trespassing/ Employees Only' sign," Joe thought as he started to collect his gear. "I bet he parked there to sleep off an all-night binge drinking outing. I better check this out before calling the police."

Joe could feel his heart pounding in his chest and he became fearful that he might pass out as he began to make the long journey from his security hut to the back corner of the employee parking lot. One never knew how situations like this might play out or if this man had any bad intentions. Adding to his anxiety was the fact that several of the parking lot lights did not work and most of the campus was bathed in darkness. As he walked, Joe checked his pockets and felt the only weapon the company provided, a can of Mace that was so old that he doubted that anything would happen if he actually pushed the spray button. He had a company-issued radio that rarely worked when he got more than 10 feet away from the security hut. If this person had any ill will, Joe hoped that he could run back across the parking lot and get close enough to his security desk in order to use his radio to call for help before too much harm came to him.

As Joe approached the pickup truck, the mystery man rolled down his window and said, "Good morning, officer. I think I am in the right place. Is this the JED Company?"

"Yes," Joe said hesitantly as his fingers gripped the can of Mace in his pocket. "Who might you be and why are you here?"

"My name is Jim Brown and I am the new vice president for this part of the company," the man said as he showed Joe his company ID. "My first day is today and I thought I would get here early to observe our employees as they arrive. One can tell a lot about the culture and morale of the workers by watching the body language of people as they get out of their cars and enter the building."

Joe looked over Jim's credentials and visibly relaxed. "My name is Joe and I have worked here for over 20 years. Based on my experiences, the first car will probably not arrive for another 45 minutes or so. I can't remember the last time anyone got here early. I have a thermos of hot coffee in the security office. Do you want to come in and warm up a bit while you wait? The sun won't be up for another 20 minutes, so it won't do much good sitting in the dark."

Jim thanked Joe for the invitation and followed him to the small security hut. "I noticed that many of the parking lot lights don't work," said Jim. "The safety of our employees will be one of my top priorities going into this job. It is hard to build trust and collaboration if the employees feel unsafe. I will have someone out here by the end of the week to start fixing those lights. What else can I do to help you with your job, Officer Joe?"

Joe shared how his only protection was an expired can of Mace and how his radio did not work most of the time. Jim wrote these things down in a notebook he kept in his shirt pocket. After taking another sip, Jim said, "This is great coffee. I noticed you bring your own thermos. Do you not like the coffee that the company provides?"

Officer Joe began to chuckle. "I can't get a working radio. Do you think the company would supply coffee? As far as I can tell, the company's motto is to provide the bare bone necessities that allow the workers to get their jobs done... no more, no less." After taking another sip of coffee, the security officer added, "I hope you don't mind me saying... but you don't seem to be cut from the same cloth as our previous bosses."

"How so?" asked Jim.

"Well, for one thing, you have said more to me this morning than our past three leaders, combined. Also, you look and act like you could be one of us... one of the workers. Not a vice president. It will be interesting to see how your staff responds to someone who is quite different than what they have grown accustomed to working for."

Officer Joe was correct that the employees did not arrive any earlier than was absolutely necessary. By the time the first car arrived, Jim had returned to his pickup truck and watched the masses shuffle their way into the office building. "This group might be mistaken for the cast of *The Walking Dead*," he thought. "It is going to be a genuine challenge to bring this place back to life." When Jim was hired for this V.P. position, his new boss explained the situation to be pretty dire. This part of the business was in a tailspin with customers leaving at an alarming rate, employee morale lower than all of the other divisions, accidents and quality defects were on the rise, and profits were declining rapidly. Jim's new boss said that he wanted Jim to shake things up and get this part of the company on a path toward achieving "excellence," whatever that meant.

Eventually, Jim left his truck and made his way toward his new office. His administrative assistant met him at the entrance and introduced herself as Judy White. "This morning, you will spend most of your time in Human Resources filling out a bunch of paperwork," said Judy. "Then, I have you scheduled the rest of the day meeting with members of your staff so you can share with them what you want them to do and they can begin working on your priorities."

"Actually," said Jim, "once I get done with the HR paperwork, I have some errands to run. Then, I would like to spend the rest of the day introducing myself to the people who get the work done. Let my staff know that when I am in their department, I would be happy to have them join me as I go around and introduce myself to each and every employee."

Later that evening, Officer Joe arrived to begin his next watch and did his usual routine of clocking in and putting his gear into his locker. "Hey Joe," said one of his colleagues who had just completed his shift and was about to leave. "There is a box in the security room with your name on it."

"Thanks," said Joe. "I wonder what that is all about."

Joe got the rest of his gear on and walked over to the security hut. He opened up the box and a tear came to his eye as he looked inside. There were several new cans of Mace, a new radio for each security guard with a panic button that would instantly call the police from anywhere on the company campus, and an industrial coffee maker along with several filters and coffee blends. A note was attached to the coffee maker that read, "Thanks for the cup of coffee and the chat this morning. We depend on you and the rest of the security staff to keep things safe around here. The least we can do is make sure you have the proper tools to do your job. Let me know which blend of coffee you like best and I will make sure it is stocked in the security supply cabinet. Jim"

The next day, Jim parked in the same spot at the back of the empty employee lot and walked over to the security hut. Officer Joe invited him into the small office, poured him a cup of coffee and thanked him for the package. "You do know that there is a parking space near the entrance with your name on it, don't you?" asked Joe. "You don't have to park in the back of the lot."

"Yeah, I know," said Jim. "My plan is to turn that parking spot as well as my staff's parking places into reserved parking for customers when they visit. I want every employee to know that our customers come first and then the people who are doing the actual work meeting the needs of our customers should have the next priority in parking spaces."

"Hmm..." said Joe as he thought out loud. "I can't decide if you are serious about changing the culture around here or if you are just plain nuts. I hope you know what you are getting yourself into because I am not sure if this company is ready for someone like you."

Later that day, Jim thought about Officer Joe's words as he sat in his first meeting with his staff and listened to what was turning into a giant gripe session.

"I don't understand," said Linda Parks, the director of purchasing. "You want me to buy coffee for the security staff? The next thing you'll be wanting is coffee for the whole office. Are you trying to spend us out of business in your first week?"

"And why were you talking directly to my employees yesterday afternoon?" asked Susan Jones, the director of operations. "Do you have any idea how disruptive that was and how much our productivity dropped? We have enough problems with all of our bad luck dealing with quality problems, equipment failures, and who knows what else. We can't afford random disruptions caused by the boss walking around. Next time, please talk to me first before creating chaos with our workers."

"And you want us to fix all of the parking lot lights by the end of the week?" asked David O'Dell, the director of facilities, with an incredulous tone in his voice. "Do you know what that will do to my budget? I've got plans for every nickel if I am to meet all of my objectives for the year. I was told by your predecessor that if I missed even one of my goals, I would not get a bonus or a raise and I might be fired. I have a family to feed."

This went on for 28 minutes when Jim finally had had his fill. "That is enough!" said Jim with a firm, commanding voice. "It is becoming clear to me that you all have no idea how to effectively lead an organization." Jim could see the invisible walls of defense immediately go up, so he softened his tone. "Look, it is not your fault. I was hired into this position to 'shake things up' and I plan to start with us, this team, and how we lead our organization." He turned to his director of operations and said, "I looked over your biography last night, Susan, and you clearly have a great deal of experience. Your employees shared with me that you are a hard worker and that you will do whatever is necessary to get our customers' needs met no matter how many problems must be overcome. Who would you say had their greatest influence on how you developed your management skills?"

Susan thought for a moment and said, "Well, I guess I would have to give the most credit to my mentor when I went into my first management position. Wait, why are we talking about this again?"

"Please bear with me for just a few more minutes," implored Jim. "Who do you think taught your mentor how to be a good manager?"

"Oh, that is easy," said Susan. "Her first boss when she first became a manager. She spoke often about his influence. Are you going to get to your point?"

"Well, I bet his first boss was taught by his first boss and he was taught by his first boss and so on and so on. Your management skills can probably be traced back to the first days of the Industrial Revolution. Now, what I am about to say next applies to each of you and please do not take this the wrong way." Jim paused for dramatic effect, "perhaps, everything you know about how to manage people... is wrong."

After a few moments of silence, the room exploded with a mixture of voices that included anger, confusion, angst, and fear. When things quieted down, Susan asked, "What do you mean by 'everything you know about how to manage people is wrong' and why should we listen to another word you are about to say? I am starting to think that I need to get my résumé updated."

"Over the past several decades, many extremely successful companies from around the world have developed an entirely new way to lead their employees," Jim explained. "They form teams throughout their organizations and then treat their workers with respect and support. And, after extensive training, these teams are then empowered to make day-to-day decisions and respond to problems quickly, on the spot, closest to the actual process. These teams are also encouraged to look for ways to improve their processes on an ongoing basis and they are given the resources to implement their ideas using proven methodologies to minimize risk."

"Wait a minute," said David, the director of facilities. "It sounds to me like you want the inmates running the asylum. The only way to keep chaos from breaking out all over the place is to manage these people with a firm hand and control every aspect of... everything. That is our job to make sure things don't go all crazy."

"And your job," said Linda, the director of purchasing, "is to tell us what you want done and how you want it done. And, as long as those commands do not interfere with my personal goals and objectives, like wasting money buying coffee for the security staff, I will do everything possible to make sure those directives are carried out."

"Alright, alright," Jim sighed with a tone of defeat. "In the short term, until we are able to patch a few holes in this ship and get out of crisis mode, I will make the tough decisions. However, keep in mind that my vision of shifting from managing to leading and utilizing empowered employee teams will always be my long-term objective. Also, I would like to sit down with each of you and review your goals and objectives. Don't be surprised if several of these get changed or done away with altogether." Jim got up from his chair and pulled out a $100 bill from his billfold and tossed it out onto the table in front of Linda. "The coffee for the security staff is on me," he said as he left the room indicating that the meeting was over.

PRACTICAL APPLICATIONS

This first chapter of the story portion of this book introduces us to Jim Brown, an outsider who was hired to "shake things up" in order to turn around a failing business. He comes into the position with a different definition of leadership compared to what was in place in the past. His goal is to elevate the workers (signifying their importance) and move toward collaboration and teamwork. He and his directors are there to help support the people who are closest to the process. This way of thinking is completely foreign to his staff and signals to them that their world is about to be turned upside down. Why is Jim willing to endure the difficult transformation of the culture (putting his own job at risk) in order to begin a long journey from despair to excellence? This is a question that organizational leaders have wrestled with for decades.

Early in my own career, an executive at General Electric, who was also one of my mentors, shared with me a story that impacted the way I viewed the world of management and started my quest to understand how processes, people, culture, and leadership intertwine to impact the way things get done. The year was 1987 and U.S.-based companies were scrambling to try and figure out how Japanese manufacturers went from making junk to providing superior quality products in just a few decades. Throughout the 1970s, U.S. company executives rationalized this tidal wave of innovative, long-lasting products being produced in Japan as a fluke that would soon go away. This sentiment began to change on June 24, 1980, when NBC aired a documentary titled *If Japan Can, Why Can't We?* This was a massive wake-up call that indicated to company executives around the world that what the Japanese were doing was no fluke. Soon after, companies started sending people to Japan to try and learn what they had done to become the world leader in producing outstanding quality.

The story this executive shared with me was so impactful that it would change the direction of my entire career. He had just returned from one of these fact gathering trips and had spent considerable time with a CEO of a major Japanese company. This CEO answered every question his visitor from GE had asked until the final question: "How much money do you make?"

The CEO looked at his guest with an expression of confusion and responded, "Why do you ask such a rude and embarrassing question?"

My mentor replied, "You have shown me your entire operation and answered every one of my questions. I apologize, but I asked this question to see if there was anything you were not willing to share with me. Why have you been so accommodating?"

"For many years," he replied, "we have been working to build a culture based on lifting up our team members and focusing on eliminating waste and improving processes. The rest of the world is just now waking up to what we have accomplished. It will take you decades to overcome years of bad management practices. By the time you get to where we are now, we will be decades further on our journey. You are not a threat to us."

I remember feeling a sense of anger and bewilderment after hearing this report. I naïvely thought that within a few years, all companies from around the world would be meeting the challenge and matching the performance of our Japanese counterparts. Soon after this discussion, an event occurred, and I began to realize that this would be a far more significant challenge.

AN EARLY EXAMPLE OF A BROKEN RESPONSE TO A BROKEN PROCESS

At the time of this event, I had just started as an engineer, working on the shop floor of a major manufacturing plant. A critical piece of equipment suddenly stopped working. The initial diagnosis was that one of the electric motors that operated part of the machine needed to be replaced. We did not have a spare replacement motor on site. The maintenance supervisor called around and found the correct motor at a supply shop on the other side of the city. In order to expedite the process, we paid a taxi driver to go and pick up the motor and drive it to our plant. By this point in time, the entire production line had stopped and over 500 workers were sitting idle as they waited for this machine to begin working again.

After waiting about an hour, the replacement motor arrived, was connected to the machine, wired to a power panel, and then a rather large switch was flipped to the "on" position. I remember feeling a tremendous sense of anxiety and dread as I watched a puff of smoke billow out of this replacement motor indicating to all of us that the motor had just been fried. We discovered that the electrical panel that the motor had been wired into had been mislabeled and an incorrect amount of power surged through the wires resulting in immediate and permanent failure. We then had to rush a second motor to the plant via another expensive taxi ride. This second motor was installed and several people checked the wiring before the power switch was flipped to the "on" position a second time. To the great relief of everyone involved, the motor started working but, to our horror, the machine it was connected to did not budge. The real problem, it turned out, was not the motor (and never had been) but the gear box that was attached to the motor. A gear box is exactly what it sounds like; a metal box full of gears to transfer the power of the motor to the machine. The box is usually full of oil to help reduce the friction and heat generated by a bunch of gears rotating at high speeds. As soon as we opened this particular gear box, we noticed two things. First, that the box was void of any oil and apparently had been empty of oil for a fairly long time. We knew this because of the second realization; the gears inside of the box were worn down to the point that none of them worked.

Of course, we did not have a spare gear box on site, so we dispatched the taxi a third time to go and pick up a replacement. Once it arrived, the maintenance folks quickly got it installed and the machine started working. The total time that the production line was down came to a little over 6 hours. The warehouse was only big enough to hold 4 hours of inventory (the product we produced was quite large). No shipments could be made for over 2 hours, resulting in significant cost to the company and many unhappy customers.

The next day, all of the people who were involved and their bosses were invited to a meeting to discuss what had happened. The plant manager (my boss's boss's boss) walked into the conference room and began the meeting by saying, "Who are we going to fire? This fiasco cannot go unpunished!" Immediately, everyone's defenses went up and the blame game began. "It wasn't our fault," said one of the department managers. "It wasn't us," said another. This went on for several minutes until the manager of operations spoke. "Look," he said. "It is impossible to predict when these types of failures will occur. We got unlucky yesterday and we might be unlucky again. This problem took 6 hours to fix and we only had 4 hours of inventory. Now that we have discovered a 6-hour problem, I propose that we expand the warehouse and add 50% more inventory. This will make sure we are better prepared the next time something like this happens." Everyone held their breath as they waited to hear the plant manager's response. "Hmmm…" he said as he went deep into thought. "That sounds reasonable. Okay, we won't fire anyone today but let's make sure this never happens again!"

After everyone hurried out of the conference room, my boss and I were the only ones left. "That was a ridiculous meeting," I remember saying.

"How so?" asked my boss.

"We did not solve anything. We did not discuss a spare parts strategy, how the power panel was mislabeled, and why the gear box was out of oil. This is a very broken process, it had nothing to do with bad luck and it will happen again. Why didn't we spend our time discussing ways to fix and improve the process?"

"Sometimes, it is better to keep your head down and survive to work another day," said my boss as he got up and left the room. And that was the end of our discussion. It was at that point I decided to change career paths and begin this journey into discovering how organizations achieve excellence.

DEFINING A NEW NORMAL OF LEADERSHIP

In the spring of 2018, in order to prepare for a keynote speech I was about to give at a conference that Virginia Tech University was hosting, I asked the following question on social media: "If you had one word to describe the *main* ingredient to sustain and expand an improvement initiative, what would it be?" Over 100,000 people participated in providing feedback. I took all of the words that were supplied and created a word cloud (the size of the word indicates how many times that word was submitted). The results are shown in Figure 1.1.

FIGURE 1.1
Word Cloud of Responses.

Take notice of the two largest words: Leadership and Commitment. These were followed by: Culture and Buy-in. You may also notice words like: Engagement, People, Communication, Trust, and Vision. These are all words associated with questions such as: "How do we improve our organization's culture? Why won't my leaders fully and wholeheartedly commit to something that seems so obvious to many of us trying to make a difference? What will it take to get my boss to fully buy-in to allowing teams of employees the opportunity to improve the way things are done (and at the same time, how do we get the employees to trust us and fully buy-in as well)?"

It is interesting that "Leadership" and "Commitment" had similar results. This reminds me of the old joke that when making breakfast, the hen is involved but the pig is committed. Commitment means completely tearing down all of the old ways and defining a new "normal" of how things are done at every level within the organization. Unfortunately, many managers think that it is sufficient to do the bare minimum and try to fake their way to achieving excellence. They might allow a couple of teams to be formed (with no real authority to change anything), or spend some money on training (but not attending the classes themselves since they are so busy or it is beneath them), or ask their employees for ideas on how to improve (with little to no resources dedicated to implementing these ideas). All they are doing is creating a flimsy façade of excellence that crumbles at the first sign of trouble.

Unfortunately, the CEO from Japan back in 1987 may have been correct in his assessment of how difficult it would be to overcome years of bad management practices. Three decades have passed since that meeting, and while some progress has been made, there is still much to do. For example, non-manufacturing organizations (hospitals, government agencies, non-profits, and service providers) are just now getting started on their journeys to achieve excellence and do not yet realize how much change is required. Hopefully, the lessons contained within this book will help accelerate these improvements and begin to create a "new normal" when defining leadership.

2

Leadership, Direction, and Process Improvement

It will be difficult to overcome 100 years of bad management practices

THE STORY OF FRANK SMITH

Meanwhile, at a similar office complex located 152 miles away, Frank Smith pulled into his parking space outside of another one of the JED, Inc. divisions. He was able to maneuver his expensive sports car so that it barely touched the sign reading, "Parking Spot for V.P. Frank Smith… All others will be towed!" He exited his car and headed for a private entrance and was able to enter his office without enduring the aggravation of talking to any of his underlings. After taking a sip of coffee that is always waiting for him at his desk, he scanned his e-mails and noticed one from the previous evening. "Hmmm… it appears that we lost power last night," he thought as he read the message. "The phone systems went down and we were unable to conduct any business for several hours. Someone must be held accountable for this disaster!" Frank tried to calm his rage as he began to imagine how damaging this outage would be to his personal performance measurements. "And just when we have been asked to launch a new push to achieve 'excellence,'" he thought. "Get the staff together!" he yelled to his administrative assistant. "I want a full report on what happened with the power outage last night and who is going to pay for this incompetence!"

Later that morning, Frank blasted his way into the conference room located near his office and banged the door shut. His staff did not dare look up and each hoped they would get through this meeting without having to say anything. "What happened last night?!?" yelled Frank. After a few moments of silence, Frank slammed his fist on the table and said, "Someone better speak up or I swear, I will find a way to get rid of every single one of you."

"We did an investigation," stammered the director of facilities. "And it appears that a storm went through and one of our power lines was hit by lightning. The power surge blew through several of our circuits and fried a couple of our breaker panels. Of course, with all of the budget cuts, we did not have any spares. It took us a while to get all of the necessary parts and replace the panels. It really wasn't anyone's fault per se and our maintenance staff did an outstanding job getting us back up and running as fast as they did."

"What the..." Frank spat out as his rage was on full display. "Are you trying to tell me that we were unable to meet our customers' needs for several hours and it was nobody's fault? We have been asked to achieve excellence in everything we do. This is not excellence! We must send a message to our workforce that this is absolutely unacceptable. I am a reasonable person. Instead of firing someone, I expect the person who oversees our electrical systems to be sent home for at least 2 weeks without pay and I want – no, I demand that 100 lightning rods be installed by the end of the week to make sure that this never happens again."

"We already took a look at what we could do to protect the systems and we think four or five rods would be sufficient along with a surge protection system," said the director of facilities with a great deal of hesitancy in his voice. "We could also use some spare parts," he whispered dreading the impact of Frank's fury.

"I guess you did not hear me," yelled Frank. "One hundred lightning rods installed by the end of the week or heads will roll!" Frank walked around the conference room and after a minute of silence he looked at each person sitting around the table and softly spoke, "I am not sure you all are on board with our goals of achieving excellence. I expect that the next time a problem shows up, you will come to me with what went wrong and who will be held accountable. We need to make sure everyone in this organization understands that employment in this company is not guaranteed and that we expect all of our employees to always do good quality work so we can be the best! That includes each of you sitting around this table. Am I making myself perfectly clear?" Frank then dismissed the group but asked the director of quality, Bill Mixer, to stay behind. The group quickly left the room doing everything they could to avoid making eye contact with their boss.

"Bill," said Frank as he spoke to his quality manager, "the first area we need to focus on in order to be excellent is our quality metrics. Right now, the number of errors caused by our employees is way too high. I want a plan on my desk by the end of the week on how we are going to bring the number of errors down."

"Do you have a goal in mind? What do you think the quality needs to be in order to qualify for being recognized as excellent?" asked the director of quality.

"I don't know," said Frank, "and I really do not care. We just need to be better than all of the other divisions. Let's shoot for 98% good but we may need to raise that higher if any of the other divisions get close to that number."

"I am not sure that is possible..." said Bill with a bit of fear creeping into his voice. "Currently, we are at 84% and for years this number hasn't changed that much. I can't imagine any plan that will get us to 98% that won't require significant time and cost."

"Hey, don't worry," said Frank in a soothing tone as he patted Bill on his back. "If you can't come up with a plan by the end of the week like I am asking, then you won't need to be concerned since you will be out on the street looking for a new job. Got it? No more excuses."

Later that day, Frank was scanning his long list of e-mails and marveling at how important he must be to have so many messages piled up. He ignored his phone ringing until his administrative assistant yelled, "The president of our division is on line 1. You might want to pick that up."

"Hey boss," Frank answered. "Yes, we had a small problem yesterday that shut down our systems but don't worry, I have everything under control. I personally put together an action plan that identified the problem and who will be held accountable. I have also put into place a set of corrective actions that will guarantee that this problem will not happen again in the future." After a short pause, Frank said, "Thanks, boss. I appreciate the words of encouragement." As Frank hung up the phone he thought with a smile, "The boss knows how to recognize excellence."

PRACTICAL APPLICATIONS

This chapter introduces us to Frank Smith. Frank is a compilation of every bad manager I have encountered over the years. His entire focus is on doing what is best to promote his own career and how he can take any situation and spin it for his own benefit. As a 'manager,' he wants to control every situation and uses fear to make sure everyone in the organization does his bidding. This will lead to hiding bad information, faking data, and the unwillingness to highlight problems. The first step to making improvements happen is to admit that there is a need to change. When the organization is afraid to share their concerns, the chance for improvement diminishes greatly... and the façade of excellence begins to crumble.

I have seen several examples of bad management over the years. For instance, I was a first-time manager when the practice of eliminating the bottom 10% of each department in an organization on an annual basis was put into place. This edict moved us in the opposite direction to what the Japanese were doing. Each year, we were asked to rank our employees from best to worst and then fire the bottom 10%. At the time, I was leading a group of engineers, some of whom had Masters degrees in their area of expertise. The people I had to remove, in some cases, were much better and more qualified than those who were in the top 90% of other departments (of course, I was biased since I had mentored many of these folks... as were all of the other departmental managers biased about their employees). This created great resentment between departments, which formed and strengthened silo walls.

This practice also generated tremendous amounts of fear within the department. I remember one point in time when I had an open position to be filled and asked several of my employees to participate in the interviewing process. After talking to all of the candidates, these employees wanted me to hire the applicant that I had ranked as being at the bottom of the list. I asked them why they had ranked this awful candidate so high. Their response: "Why would we want to hire someone who might be better than us? That would push us down closer to the bottom 10% and put our jobs into jeopardy." At least they were honest with me. Of course, when we did fill this position, there was no incentive to help the new person (or any other member of the department for that matter)... the opposite of teamwork.

Some might think that Frank, in the story part of this chapter, is a bit harsh. Unfortunately, I have witnessed managers who were far, far more brutal to their employees and used fear to try to motivate. Many companies have daily production meetings to discuss all of the things that went wrong the day before. Some of the employees, who participated in these meetings, have shared with me over the years that they had three goals when attending these slug fests. First, do not get fired. Second, say anything to deflect any problems to another department or employee in order to protect your own career status and the careers of their co-workers. Third, try to survive with your dignity intact. Unfortunately, too many times, I have seen people leave these types of meetings with tears streaming down their cheeks after being reamed by their organization's manager for something that was completely outside of their control. So much fear is created in these meetings that most of the problems are never discussed and never solved. Much of the time is spent trying to shift the blame to others with little focus on improving anything.

Even the practice of using goals and objectives to motivate employees can be considered an ancient, ineffective management practice. When a manager sets a goal for one of their employees, what he or she is really saying is, "If you miss this goal, something bad will happen. I am not sure what that will be, but you can rest assured that it will be painful." The next chapter will go into the ineffectiveness of goals and objectives in more depth.

THREE DIMENSIONS TO IMPROVE IN ORDER TO ACHIEVE EXCELLENCE

How does an organization achieve excellence with all of these headwinds? There are three distinct areas that must be dealt with in order to begin an improvement initiative, accelerate the changes, and then sustain the gains (Figure 2.1).

First Circle – Processes: There are many books written about how to improve processes so we will only touch on this area. Of the three circles, I believe that this is actually the easiest. Many experts can teach anyone in an organization how to do a process map, for example, or how to get to the root cause of a problem. It is much more difficult to convince a manager that they need to change their ways and become a leader.

Second Circle – Leadership: As you can tell from the title of this book, this is the circle we will be spending the most time on. Getting leaders on board is also the most difficult part of any improvement initiative. I have heard statements from improvement professionals that drip with frustration. Statements such as: "Let's start at the bottom

FIGURE 2.1
Venn Diagram of Excellence.

and work our way up through the organization and then maybe our executives will get on board (rarely happens)." Or, "Our boss is supportive of the improvements as long as he (or she) doesn't have to do anything different (or participate in any way)." And my favorite, "As soon as we show how much money we will save, I bet our boss will embrace the improvement efforts." However, savings can be difficult to calculate with the exception of reducing headcount, which will eliminate the very employees (or their friends) who are on the improvement teams. Of course, if this happens, the trust will be broken and the improvement efforts will instantly come crashing down.

Third Circle – Direction: This circle is an area that most managers spend weeks and weeks of their time working on and rarely does it have the expected impact. Many organizations have a "strategic planning" session every year. When I went through this process as a manager, we would spend considerable time and energy working up a "dog and pony show" presentation and hope that when we presented the information to the top leaders, our careers stayed intact. Once (and if) we survived the planning process, we would breathe a huge sigh of relief and then put our strategic plan on a shelf somewhere and not look at it again until the following year (when the process started all over again). This is an area that needs to be completely revamped. Leaders in properly run organizations that utilize empowered teams will actually be spending more of their time in this direction circle. There seems to be a great deal of confusion as to what is meant by Mission, Vision, Strategy, and Values; how they are different; and what their purposes are in helping motivate employees toward excellence (yes, understanding and applying these four directional components is essential to achieving excellence). We will cover this circle in-depth throughout this book.

Over the years, I have had the privilege of working with several forward-thinking organizations, many of which have come close to matching the performance bar set by the Japanese. Each of these companies had solid leaders throughout the organization and they understood the importance of all three of the circles listed above. They realized that their role was to do everything possible to help the people, who executed the processes, meet the needs of their customers. The leaders set up teams throughout the organization and invested time and money into training and mentoring their employees, designing (with significant input from the workers) robust processes, and providing resources to help the teams achieve improvements and solve problems on a continuous basis. These leaders also understood the importance of seeing strings of processes as systems that required each part to work seamlessly together and that no one was successful unless everyone was successful. These organizations achieved performance results that set them apart from their competitors and significantly increased their chances for long-term job security for their employees.

Another example of companies that understand what it takes to achieve excellence can be found in the pages of *IndustryWeek* magazine. This periodical has been around for many years and it was one of the key references we used when I was at GE to learn about this new field of continuous process improvement in the 1980s. *IndustryWeek* continues to lead the way on reporting about new trends in manufacturing and technology to this day. They conduct an annual "*IndustryWeek* – Best Plants" competition and any North American manufacturing plant that meets the eligibility requirements can apply. For the past several years, I have been a judge in this competition and when looking at the data that has been collected, there are distinct trends and conclusions that can be made. Most of the organizations that have achieved superior performance results (customer satisfaction, safety, quality, delivery, etc.) highlight throughout their presentations the use and dependence on high-performance employee teams. These groups go much deeper than simple problem-solving teams. In many cases, these teams of workers are empowered to make decisions, utilize resources, and even help in the hiring process. Several of these companies also highlight the fact that they have been awarded a "Best Place to Work" honor from their state or industry indicating that the morale of the workforce is consistently high and the employees are proud to be a part of the organization.

There is significant evidence that cultures can be changed, leaders can be retrained, employees can be empowered, and customers can be delighted. It is only a matter of time before all organizations wake up to this new way of doing things.

3

The Misuse of Management by Objectives

The fear and anxiety created by the misuse of goals contribute to the façade of excellence

THE STORY OF FRANK SMITH

Tick... Tock... Tick... Tock...

The antique grandfather clock, located down the hall from Bill Mixer's bedroom, seemed especially noisy this particular night.

Tick... Tock... Tick... Bong!... Bong!

2:00 a.m. Bill stared up at the ceiling as his wife slept peacefully next to him. She had no idea of Bill's anguish as he kept replaying Frank Smith's words from earlier that day: "If you can't come up with a plan by the end of the week like I am asking, then you won't need to be concerned since you will be out on the street looking for a new job!" Bill's 17-year-old daughter had applied to and had been accepted by several expensive universities. His son was three years younger and had already started talking about wanting to go to college as well. "How are we going to pay for their education if I am out of a job?" thought Bill. "It will be impossible to cover their costs and have anything left for retirement. I have got to come up with a plan to make our quality metrics improve from 84% to 98% and meet my boss's expectations."

Tick... Tock... Tick... Tock...

"If I had a couple of years and an unlimited budget, then maybe it would be possible to buy our way to better quality. But that isn't going to happen... at least not under Frank's watch. What to do? What to do?" Bill felt a bead of sweat roll down his forehead as the stress of the moment began to take a toll. "Hmmm… Maybe we could start hiding parts that have defects. We could put them into the trash dumpsters and never record the errors." Bill's conscience began to kick in and he thought, "No. I couldn't allow that to happen… plus our audit programs might detect the discrepancies in the data." Bill let out a long sigh. "Maybe we could just look the other way and send the defective parts to our customers. I could eliminate most of the inspectors and only keep the ones with bad eyesight or who are bad at catching defects. We could eliminate most of the lights at the inspection stations as well. That would cause them to miss most of the errors and our quality data will improve dramatically. Of course, it will not take long for our customers to start flooding us with product returns and complaints. I might survive for a few weeks, but the long-term prospects would look pretty bleak. No. Not the answer. What to do? What to do?"

Tick… Tock… Tick…

"I've got it!" thought Bill with such enthusiasm that he almost woke up his wife. "What if we just redefine what an error is and how we record our defects? If we only report the most severe problems… say the ones that might cause harm to our customers, then our numbers would improve dramatically. We would easily be over the 98% goal Frank is looking for." Bill quickly wrote his idea down on a notepad that was on the nightstand by his bed and rolled over and finally went to sleep.

Later that week, at their staff meeting, Frank Smith asked his director of quality to present his plan to meet the new goal.

"I believe we have been too hard on ourselves," began Bill as he avoided eye contact with his peers on the staff. He could already feel them judging him. "We are counting all of our mistakes, and the quality metrics we send to our corporate offices incorporate all of this data. While the bulk of these defect types are important to track internally, the corporate executives and the outside world really only care about those problems that might cause liabilities with our customers. If you look at the chart on the screen (Figure 3.1), defect type 4 is the only one that could possibly hurt or, in rare cases, kill one of our customers. I propose that we recalculate our quality data and only include defect type 4. This would result in a quality metric of 98.3%."

Frank stared at Bill and did not speak right away. The rest of the staff looked at Bill with a mixture of expressions that ranged from disbelief to outright horror. The silence was broken when finally, a single pair of hands began to clap… slowly at first and then picking up speed.

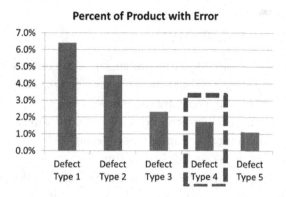

FIGURE 3.1
Chart of Defects.

When the rest of the staff realized that it was Frank who was clapping, they too began to clap. "That is what I call 'out of the box' thinking!" said Frank enthusiastically. "Bill clearly understands what it takes to achieve excellence. I hope the rest of you can learn from Bill's approach to meeting our goals and objectives."

"But won't it be obvious to the corporate folks that something unusual is going on if all of a sudden our quality goes from 84% to 98% overnight?" asked the director of facilities.

Frank's smile began to tighten as he replied to this criticism. "I am beginning to think that you are not a team player." He paused for a moment and then added, "Actually, our facilities manager has a point. Let's remove only one defect type each month so the data will not jump up too quickly. That should keep the executives from prying into the numbers."

"Doesn't this break some sort of ethics rules?" asked the director of finance.

Frank's patience was clearly starting to be tested. "Look. One of the things I remember learning from a previous boss of mine, who was also a great mentor, is that managers, who do well in their career, are those who are good at spinning the numbers. There are many examples throughout history of executives who were able to get huge promotions and bonuses just before the business they were running went belly up. They understood the importance of telling a good story even if it means sweeping some of the problems under the rug. I hope the rest of you follow Bill's lead and come up with creative ways to show the world how excellent we are!"

THE STORY OF JIM BROWN

On the other side of the state, Jim Brown sat in his office with a pile of sealed manila envelopes stacked on his desk. "Judy!" yelled Jim to his administrative assistant. "What are these envelopes?"

"Those are the annual performance goals of your direct reports. You asked me to get them for you from Human Resources."

"Why are the envelopes sealed?" asked Jim.

"Hmmm, I am not sure why you are asking that," replied Judy as she walked into Jim's office. "The people who have sat in your chair before have always made it a point to keep everyone's performance goals and objectives secret from everyone else. They explained that this is personal information and should only be seen by the employee and the boss."

"It seems that it would be difficult for my staff to work together as a team if they do not know how everyone has defined success. What if there are conflicts that arise between two or more people's goals?" asked Jim. "That would lead to confusion, finger pointing, and a breakdown in trust which would cause silos to form around the various departments."

"Ha! That is a good one, boss. No disrespect, but I don't think this staff has a team bone in their bodies," said Judy. "The previous V.P. spoke often about how every member of this staff should be hungry for promotions and that each person was in a competition to take this job when he left. You can imagine how disappointed everyone was when they hired an outsider and no one got promoted."

"Ah, that explains why they have been so vocally hostile in our staff meetings. Well, I think it is time to change a few things around here." Jim, ripped open each of the sealed envelopes, stacked the papers onto his desk, and threw the envelopes into the trash. It did not take long for him to find major conflicts between the objectives of several of his staff. "No wonder they do not support each other. There is no way for everyone to win at the same time. And, few of these goals are focused on our customers, employees, or generating profits. This has got to change."

Later that day, Jim decided to walk around the campus and observe how things got done to meet the needs of their customers. At one point on his walk, he stopped to observe, from afar, an inspector measuring parts contained in a large bin. The employee picked up a part, measured one of the dimensions, looked at a chart, and then without writing anything down, he threw the part back into the bin. This happened several times until finally, the measurement on one of the parts seemed to be satisfactory and that was the information that got recorded. "Wait, did I just see that inspector skew the data by not recording the bad parts?" thought Jim with disgust. "Maybe I did not see that quite right. I better dig a bit deeper before jumping to conclusions."

He continued his walk and overheard a conversation that took place between a different quality inspector and one of the supervisors. "Hey boss," the inspector said, "I am going on vacation next week. Do you want me to fill out all of the quality reports for next week's production before I leave?" "Wait a minute," thought Jim, "How would it be possible to record data for something that has not happened yet?!?"

Jim was starting to realize why there was a significant disconnect between their customers' experiences with major quality issues and the internal data that showed everything was fine. He continued his walk and noticed a banner that read "Congratulations! For the Third Month in a Row, this Group Has the Best Quality of this Division!!!" "Finally," thought Jim. "Maybe I have found an area of the business that has their act together." He began walking through the department when he noticed an inspector working diligently at his desk. He was busy filling out a quality report that indicated that they had only two errors for the entire day. However, there was a paper napkin covered in tick marks next to the report. "How are things going?" asked Jim.

"Umm... Good, I think," said the inspector while trying to quickly cover up the napkin.

"I see you are filling out the quality report for the day. What is the purpose of the paper napkin?"

The inspector's face turned crimson red as he stammered, "Well, um, the paper napkin, um, that is the number of errors we actually had today. I keep these napkins in my personal filing cabinet."

"Wait, I thought the quality report was used to capture all of the errors," replied Jim. "Why is it necessary to keep two sets of reports?"

"Well, to be honest, if I record too many errors on the official report, the supervisor of the area yells at everybody," said the inspector. "I don't like to see my buddies get yelled at, so I only record the most significant errors on the official report. Whew! You don't know how good it feels to finally tell someone what is really going on. I have hated my job and frankly have not felt too good about myself for many years." The inspector knew he was talking to the new V.P. of the business and fully expected to be reprimanded or even fired on the spot.

"Thank you for being open and honest with me," replied Jim in a soothing voice. "I don't blame you for trying to protect your friends. Fear can cause people to do wacky things. I will speak to all of the supervisors and explain that we need to celebrate errors, not hide them. The only way we will be able to improve is to admit that we have problems and we must have accurate data to help us if we ever hope to achieve excellence."

Jim went back into the office area and asked his staff to shut down all activities 30 minutes before quitting time so he could hold a meeting with all of the employees that afternoon. Susan Jones, the director of operations, and the rest of the staff reluctantly agreed but wanted to make sure that the lost productivity would not impact their performance goals. The meeting had to be held in the parking lot to accommodate everyone and Jim stood on a ladder with a bullhorn so everyone could see and hear him.

"I wanted to take a few minutes and share with you some observations I have made since starting here a few days ago," began Jim. He had with him a stack of quality reports he had collected and held them up for everyone to see. "These quality reports are not worth the paper they are written on." He then set the bullhorn down and ripped the stack of reports into pieces. There was a mixture of reaction from the crowd ranging from gasps to laughter. Jim threw the torn up reports into a big trash can that was at the base of the ladder and picked up the bullhorn. "We need to start over and be honest with ourselves regarding how poor our performance is if we have any hope of turning this business around. I want us to stop hiding our problems and begin to work together to try to figure out how to permanently fix these issues. Let's celebrate when a problem occurs and then try to figure out how to make sure that it never happens again." There were a few smatterings of applause as the group of employees tried to understand exactly what all of this meant. Jim continued, "I know I am new here and I do not have all of the answers. That is why I am asking all of you for your help. I hope that you all want to work for a company that is built on sound fundamentals like taking care of our customers, respecting our co-workers, and stabilizing and then growing our business into something that will last and provide long-term job security. I want this to be a place you all look forward to coming to work each day and that you would be proud to show off to your families. Please hang with me as we make some changes and I look forward to hearing your ideas on ways we can be better." A few employees began to clap and as Jim's message began to sink in, more joined. Soon, the entire parking lot erupted in applause and cheers. Jim observed that his staff did not look happy with this turn of events. Susan, his director of operations, was so disgusted with this speech that Jim noticed that she walked over to her car, got in, and drove away.

PRACTICAL APPLICATIONS

Unfortunately, each of the examples in the story above regarding skewing and faking data is based on events I have personally witnessed throughout my career. This includes all of the actions taken by the inspectors as well as the ideas Bill thought of to achieve 98%, such as hiding defective parts, changing the rejection criteria to improve the acceptance rate, and even the strategy of only reporting defects that would hurt or kill the customer in order to artificially improve the results. It has become apparent over the years that the misuse of goals and objectives can cause people to do ridiculous things and destroy any hope for achieving real excellence.

To be clear, it is critically important to track data and measure progress toward achieving excellence as an organization. Objectives can be used to help define a common path toward a vision and define what success for the organization looks like (and help determine when it is appropriate to celebrate as a team). However, a management technique that has been in place for decades is the practice of giving specific goals to an employee as a part of their annual performance review. This is usually meant to do two things; through the use of fear, motivate the employee to complete a task (achieve the goal or you will not get a raise or maybe even be fired) and share a sliver of the strategic plan as far as what is important to the executives of the company (this year, we want to focus on xyz, so here are your goals). This is known as Management by Objectives (MBO) and can be viewed as one of the deep-rooted management practices that will be difficult to overcome in order to set up a new way of leading. As more and more companies move away from using MBOs, they have discovered that there is a far better way to motivate and engage employees, without the use of fear. Later in this book, we will discuss what I like to call "enthusiastic productivity," the opposite of using fear to motivate.

To illustrate how damaging Management by Objectives can be, imagine what would happen if a football coach tried to motivate the players the same way a company manager does; through the use of an annual goals and objectives process.

CHARACTERISTICS OF A WINNING TEAM

A champion-caliber football team may not have the best athletes or the most experienced coaches. However, the players, coaches, and all of the support staff commit to a common vision of doing everything within the rules to win a championship. They train hard and practice the same play over and over in order to reduce the chance of errors (repeatable processes). The quarterback is confident that when a play is called, everyone will know exactly what to do. Many times, a pass will be thrown to a certain spot on the field because the quarterback trusts that the receiver will know exactly where to go and when to turn around to catch the ball. Each player focuses on the success of the team even if that means playing in a support role. For example, when the team plays an opponent with a weak pass defense, the running back will do everything possible to protect the quarterback in order to give him more time to make a successful pass. This might mean that the running back will get few opportunities to touch the football that game and will not be able to contribute to their own personal stats. This will not be a problem since the entire team stays focused on the vision: winning a championship. The coaches will demonstrate leadership characteristics and will work with each player to grow their capabilities. The players build a strong trust with each other and their coaches, knowing that each will do their job and will help the other players whenever possible. When a play breaks down (the opposition changes the defense or a fumble occurs), the quarterback is empowered to change the play before it starts and the players are empowered to do whatever is necessary to try to gain positive yards.

USING PERSONAL GOALS INSTEAD OF TEAM GOALS

Now, imagine what would happen to the team dynamics if the coach started using Management by Objectives and told the quarterback at the beginning of the season that the only way he would be successful is if he achieved personal goals such as running the ball every play, keeping all of the play information to themselves, and not making any mistakes such as fumbling the ball or committing a penalty. The quarterback would think that these objectives would be next to impossible to achieve and give up before the first game even started. If this happens, the coach might try to compensate by throwing fear into the mix ("Meet these goals or else I will switch you out with the backup quarterback so fast it will make your head spin!"). Now imagine the same coach telling the running back that his goals were to only fumble the ball no more than twice per game, gain at least one yard per carry, and not lose his helmet between plays. This player might become complacent and not try hard to excel since the bar was set so low. In addition, what would happen if the coach told the offensive line that their goal was to not get any dirt on their uniforms, even if that meant not providing blocking protection for the other players? In each of these cases, the players would be focused on the wrong thing; meeting their own personal goals and forgetting why they are playing the game in the first place. Chaos would break out and it would be difficult for the team to win. The same thing can happen when Management by Objectives is misused in any organization.

What are some of the negatives associated with trying to manage and manipulate people through the use of setting goals and objectives (vs. providing leadership)?

- First, many goals seem arbitrary to the workers and most will assume that their objectives are significantly harder than their peers. This leads to division within the organization (the opposite of teamwork) and can cause employees to act unethically and deviously to try to hit a goal that they think is unfair.
- Second, goals can actually have the opposite impact to what was intended. If a goal is set too low or focused on the wrong things, then the organization might think they are doing well ("Look at how many goals we met") when in reality, they are falling behind their competitors. For example, a company wants to improve their delivery process. If they are currently at 2-week deliveries and have a goal to cut that time in half, they could be successful and still go out of business, especially if their competitors are already delivering the product in 2 days or less.
- And third, most improvement experts have learned over the years that it is important to focus on improving the process instead of pointing fingers at the workers. Setting goals without the ability to change and improve the process can lead to great frustration. For example, imagine if you were a truck driver and the company you work for supplied you a truck that broke down every ten miles.

Imagine how you would feel if your boss then called you into the office and said that your goal for the year was to deliver every load on time and with no delays. The driver would feel completely helpless.

How does each of these concerns about MBOs impact the organization's path toward excellence?

ARBITRARY GOALS AND FEAR

Management by Objectives is commonly used in most organizations. The fear of missing a goal can cause employees to do unexpected things, up to and including hiding information, faking data, and pushing the boundaries of unethical behavior. Most of these actions are subtle in nature and can be causing great damage without the boss (or company executives) knowing what exactly is happening until it is too late. There are many examples in today's headlines regarding companies that have suffered great losses due to employees doing senseless things in order to hit goals that were set for them by their bosses.

For example, one business gave all of their product managers a goal to lower their internal costs. They had recently bought a new robotic cell that could do the equivalent work of three manual operations with far better quality. However, none of the managers wanted to use this robotic cell because all of the costs associated with this new automation would be placed on the parts they were responsible for (these costs would come down dramatically if all of the managers shifted their production to the robotic cell, but no one wanted to be first). This expensive piece of equipment sat mostly idle and all of the parts continued to be routed through the manual operations.

In another example, a manager was told to attend, along with all of his employees, a class on how to improve processes. The class seemed to go well, and the employees enthusiastically shared several ideas on how to improve their processes. After the class was over and the employees went home, the manager walked up to me and said, "Thank you for a great class. I think everyone learned quite a bit." He paused for a few seconds and then added in a hushed voice, "You need to understand that we will not be able to implement any of the employee improvement ideas or tools you taught us. My number one goal, which my pay and bonus opportunity are directly tied into, is how much of the day my employees are utilized. If we improve our processes, then we might get done with our work faster and my employees might run out of things to do. If that is the case, then their utilization will drop and I will miss my goal. Frankly, I would rather be late on all of our orders to our customers if that means we can stay productive the entire day." Until this goal is abolished, this organization has no chance of improving.

A GOAL THAT IS TOO EASY OR TOO DIFFICULT

Another aspect of Management by Objectives that can derail striving for excellence is that a goal can limit people's imagination and creative thinking on how to get better. For example, if a metric is currently at 85% and the goal is to get to 85.1%, then the employees might not see this as all that important and end up doing the bare minimum to achieve a small amount of improvement. There is little to no incentive to think of radically different ways to do things in order to strive for excellence.

On the other hand, if the goal is deemed to be too difficult to achieve, then the employees may just throw their hands up and say that achieving that dramatic of an improvement is impossible and do nothing (or try to cheat the system like Bill, the director of quality, did in the story). They would then hope that their boss leaves before the next performance review occurs or priorities change within the business and the goal goes away (or try to fake their way through their next review).

What is a better way to achieve significant improvement? In some of my training classes, I give the participants an activity and track the amount of time it takes to accomplish the task. I then challenge them to come up with ideas on how to cut the time in half and we repeat the activity utilizing these new ideas. Most of the teams are able to easily meet or exceed this challenge. After celebrating their accomplishment, I ask them to cut the time in half again. They build on what worked in the first go around and come up with some new ideas and can usually meet or exceed this new challenge as a team. I then ask them to cut the time in half a third and maybe even a fourth time. Again, the team builds on what worked before and can usually meet or exceed this new challenge. After three or four iterations, they usually are able to cut the time from several minutes to just a few seconds. In the debrief, I ask the teams what they might have thought if I had challenged them at the beginning of the activity to cut their times by 98%. They share with me that they probably would have given up, not even tried to meet this objective since it seemed so difficult. Then I say, "Yet, you were able to achieve over 98% improvement. How did you accomplish this challenge?" Their usual answer: "Through the use of teamwork, the willingness to try new ideas, and continuous improvement, we were able to exceed even our own expectations."

EMPLOYEE PERFORMANCE VS. PROCESS PERFORMANCE

What does it mean when an employee misses a goal? Does this indicate that the employee is incompetent or lazy or a troublemaker? What if that employee works in a broken process or system and it is impossible to achieve the objective? Before judging the employee, it would be interesting to see if the boss (or anyone else) could do the job any better. Begin by blaming the process before jumping to the conclusion that it is the employee's fault (I rarely encountered an employee who came to work each day wanting to do a bad job). Every individual person possesses a unique set of skills and competencies. There are times when an employee is just not capable of achieving the expected results (assuming they have a sound process to work with). In these cases, the organization may need to provide additional training (apprenticeships) or move the employee into a different role (if available) that is better suited or redesign the process to make it less dependent on the skills of a single worker.

For example, in one business, the process was designed so that the employees had to type in a 10-digit number and print out labels in order to track where the parts were going. This was done hundreds of times throughout the day. If even one of the 10 digits was wrong, the parts would be lost and it could take hours to try to find them. The manager of the area wanted to fire all of the workers for incompetence and "not caring" about their job. In a class this manager attended, I asked all of the participants to write down a 10-digit number and pass the paper to their neighbor. I gave them 3 seconds to perform this task. The receiving person had to rewrite the number in 3 seconds and pass the paper to their neighbor. This went on for 2 minutes. Of course, while this was being done, I provided some distractions (lights going on and off, speaking to the participants, "accidentally" knocking the papers off of the desks, etc.). At the end of the activity, not a single 10-digit number matched exactly the one at the top of the paper. This was a real wake-up call for the manager that it is not the people but the process. He and the employees worked together to redesign how things were done and they came up with an entirely new process that eliminated the need to use the 10-digit numbers altogether, and the process improved significantly.

One final note about the ineffectiveness of the annual performance rating process: in today's environment where customers want things done faster and better than ever before, it is imperative that the organization stay as nimble and quick-reacting as possible. This requires a constant assessment of the current business environment and a good leader who can help the organization's teams adapt as needed. For example, in a game situation, the football coach in the analogy above will want to shift strategies depending on the current set of circumstances. This would be difficult to do if the players are focused on only meeting their personal, annual goals.

If Management by Objectives is not the answer, what can be done instead? There is a different approach to motivating employees. Everyone wants to be part of a winning team. In the example about the football players, the ultimate goal is to win the games. Throughout the season, the coach may want the players to work on improving certain skills or learn certain plays. However, the focus should be on winning. Organizations can do the same thing by building a sense of pride within the ranks. This requires communicating performance metrics to all employees; having team discussions on ways to get better every day; allowing workers at all levels to interact with customers; providing the tools and time to keep a clean, orderly, and well-lit work environment; and allowing everyone to participate in the improvement process.

As organizations migrate to a team-based model, then Management by Objectives will be replaced by tracking the rate of improvement of several customer-focused performance metrics. It is important to utilize a set of measurements that balances the needs of the customers (quality and delivery) with the needs of the employees (safety and job enhancement) and the needs of the business (profits and growth). Actually, for many of these metrics, the target will be 100% and the entire organization needs to understand the importance of working toward achieving this level of excellence. The leaders can then set "celebration points" on their journey toward achieving excellence. For example, after several improvement ideas have been implemented and the metric is consistently tracking better than it was (for instance, going from 85% to 90%), the leaders can set up a celebration to recognize the hard work done by everyone in the organization. After more ideas are implemented and the metric moves several additional percentage points higher, then the leaders can invite all of the family members to join the employees for a family day celebration. We did this at one business and had a dunking booth (dunk the leaders), clowns with balloons for the kids, a bouncy house, a great meal, and tours of the operations and offices. You could see the pride in the faces of the employees as they got a chance to show their families where they worked. Many of them pointed out the improvement ideas their teams implemented that resulted in the successes that were being celebrated.

In another example, each time we hit 100% in one or more of the three major performance metrics we tracked (Safety, Quality, and Schedule Attainment), everyone in the organization was awarded points (they could also collect points by serving on improvement teams). These points could be collected and turned in for a variety of gifts. These gifts ranged from company mugs to shirts to substantially larger items. In one example, an employee collected her points for a couple of years and turned them in for a large-screen TV. We tracked the three performance indicators in real time on large scoreboards located throughout the business. The employees asked many great questions about the metrics, which indicated that they paid attention to how the company was doing in meeting the needs of their customers.

WHY STRIVE FOR 100%?

Over the years, I have heard several comments made such as "Getting to 100% is impossible," or "What about diminishing returns going from 99% to 100%?" If this is the thinking of your managers, then achieving excellence will always be out of reach. There are several examples of organizations that have gone years without a single safety issue or accident (100% safe) or have not had a customer complaint or missed shipment (100% satisfaction). It may take some time and require a radically different set of processes and systems and a completely different way of leading, but 100% is attainable in any metric. Some will say that it will cost too much for such a small amount of return on that investment. Again, this misses the point of working toward achieving excellence (let's settle for something we know is subpar) and is not always accurate. Many of the best improvement ideas required little to no investment or minor design changes that would prevent an error from ever occurring. The Japanese have a term for this, *poka-yoke*, which translates into "mistake proofing." In other words, how can a process or part be designed so that there is only one way to accomplish the task? This means that the activity cannot be done incorrectly, resulting in 100% success.

If the organization does not use Management by Objectives, what can be done to identify the best employees? Later in this book, we will cover the importance of organizational values. My experience is that an employee who demonstrates and personifies the values that are important to achieving excellence in a team environment can be extremely valuable to the organization. The leaders' objectives will need to be focused on mentoring and growing the skills and knowledge of these team members. It is far easier to teach someone how to do a task or operate a process (or make improvements) than it is to teach them values such as teamwork, ethics, and peacemaking. In a team environment, demonstrating the right values is essential and will need to play a major role in determining pay, bonuses, and future promotional opportunities.

4

Introducing the Four Styles of Leadership

Why do some of the best leaders fail when circumstances change? Is there more than one way to lead?

THE STORY OF JIM BROWN

Jim Brown's director of operations was in a sour mood. Susan Jones poked the same piece of pasta with her fork for the third time without actually moving it off of her plate. She and her husband were celebrating their fifteenth wedding anniversary at one of the nicest restaurants in town. "Do you want to talk about it?" asked her husband.

"What? Oh... Sorry," stammered Susan. "I am not much of a date this evening. I have too much on my mind."

"Yeah, you barely touched your Lobster Bisque and you have only taken one or two bites of your favorite pasta dish. So, do you want to talk about it?" repeated her husband.

"No... not really..." A few minutes of silence passed before Susan spoke again. "It's work. I resigned this afternoon."

"What?!?" exclaimed her husband. "We just found out this week that both of our children will need braces. We depend on both of our incomes." He paused a moment as he could see the pain and anguish on his wife's face and decided that maybe he was digging a hole that might be difficult to get out of. "I'm sorry," he said as he softened his tone. "Of course, I will support whatever you think is best."

"Thanks," said Susan. "It is not official yet. I will be meeting with my boss, Jim Brown, and our human resources specialist tomorrow to submit my letter of resignation. But, I made it pretty clear in our staff meeting this afternoon that I was leaving… just before I stormed out and slammed the door."

"What happened in the staff meeting?" asked her husband.

"Oh, it is more than what happened today… this has been building for a while and what was said in the staff meeting was the last straw. Over the past couple of weeks, it has become clear to me that Jim's leadership style is completely foreign to everything I have been taught about how to manage people. He keeps talking about a new way to lead that requires getting our employees involved. I have always been taught that the boss, Jim in this case, needs to make the decisions and his staff manages the people in their departments to make sure the boss's decisions are carried out. I am really good at getting things done and managing people. He wants us to become leaders. I think this is just a way for him to shift responsibility and decision making from his shoulders to ours. And then, if something goes wrong, he can deflect the blame toward his staff."

"So, what happened today that got you to the point of resigning?" asked Susan's husband.

"Jim had the nerve to share our personal goals and objectives with the rest of the staff. These goals were meant to be private and I have worked hard over the years to persuade my previous bosses to set goals that would help promote my career. Well, all of that went up in smoke this afternoon. Jim Brown wants his staff to share objectives that are directly tied into our customers' satisfaction, the well-being of our employees, and the growth and profits of the business. He said it would help us work more like a team. We will have some individual objectives, but he wants those to be focused on our own personal development and the mentoring of our employees. How will I ever stand out and be considered for a promotion with goals like that?"

"Well, they did go outside to fill the V.P. role…" Susan shot her husband a look that clearly indicated he had said the wrong thing. "I just meant to say that maybe the executives are looking for someone with a different set of leadership skills than what you have been accustomed to working for. You can resign if you think that is best, but if you decided to stay, maybe there are some things you could learn from your new boss." This was not what Susan wanted to hear. The rest of the meal was eaten in cold, stony silence.

A few miles away, Jim Brown was busy fixing dinner when his wife, Danielle, finally got home. She had put in a long day at the local hospital where she was working as a resident so she could finish her medical training. These days were even more tiring since she was 3 months pregnant with their first child.

"Yum, I smell spaghetti for dinner," said Jim's wife.

"The best spaghetti sauce that can be poured out of a jar," said Jim with a smile. The empty jar indicated that the sauce was a generic brand. They had to watch every penny in order to make sure there were sufficient funds to pay off their school loan debts and to start buying furniture, clothes, and supplies for their future baby.

After they had eaten, Jim cleared the table and began washing the dishes. "You did not say much during dinner," Danielle said. "Is something bothering you?"

"Oh, it's work," said Jim. "One of my key staff members is planning to give me her letter of resignation tomorrow. I haven't figured out yet how to get through to my team and it is starting to take a toll. Why can't they see how powerful it will be to get all of our employees engaged in the future success of our business? The workers are the ones who are closest to the processes and if they were trained and empowered to make on-the-spot decisions, things could run so much smoother."

"Maybe that is too much of a leap for them to make after years of being told what to do," said Danielle. She walked over to one of the kitchen drawers and pulled out a pad of paper and a marker. Jim joined her at the kitchen table. She drew a line across the page and wrote the word "Dictator" on the left side and "Collaborator" on the right.

"It sounds like your staff wants you to tell them what to do and they want you to make all of the decisions," Danielle explained. "To me, that sounds like they want you to act like a dictator." She pointed to the left side of the piece of paper. "You want to focus on developing teams of workers who are trained to make on-the-spot decisions to help address problems quickly and to look for ways to improve how they do things. That sounds like collaboration to me. The problem you are having with your staff may be that the leap from dictator to collaborator is just too great for them to grasp and be comfortable with. I can see why they think you are turning their world upside down. Maybe there should be two or three gradual steps to ease them into collaboration."

Jim took Danielle's diagram and divided the line into segments by drawing four marks. He then wrote above the first mark next to the word Dictator "Boss Makes Decisions and Tells People What to Do" and above the mark next to Collaborator wrote "Fully Empowered Teams of Employees Working Together and with Boss to Achieve Excellence."

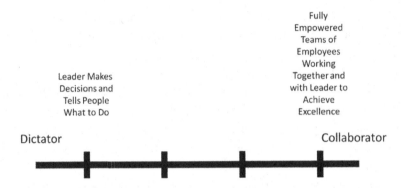

FIGURE 4.1
Dictator to Collaborator.

"The word 'Boss' seems a bit harsh," said Danielle. "I think 'Leader' is more appropriate." Jim agreed and updated the diagram (Figure 4.1).

"Hmmm..." thought Jim out loud. "What is the next step up from the 'Dictator' style of leadership? To change the culture, we need to get all of the employees to alter the way they interact with each other, begin building pride about their work, and think about the way the organization can be better in all aspects of what we do. This requires the development of ownership into the future success of the entire organization. What can I do to nudge the organization toward collaboration?"

"Simple. Ask for their input," replied Danielle. "By engaging everyone in dialogue about what can be done to make things better, it will start the wheels turning and help focus people on a brighter future. But it will be important to sincerely listen and try to implement as many of their ideas as possible. If people don't think you are sincere, this could backfire and make them even more bitter than they are now."

"That is a good point," said Jim. "While I am utilizing the dictator leadership style that my staff wants, I can start asking for their input. Plus, I can ask one or two of my staff to begin talking to some of their workers and soliciting their thoughts on ways we can make improvements to the processes they use every day. You are right that it will be important to listen and work hard to address as many of the ideas as possible if we want to continue to engage people throughout the organization."

Jim added the words "Leader Makes Decisions after Receiving Significant Input and Asks for Ideas on How to Improve" over the second hash mark on their diagram. "I think the next step would be the use of small, focused teams to solve specifically assigned problems," said Jim. "This would accomplish several things. First, the middle managers would need to relinquish small amounts of control and decision making to the teams. Second, the employees who serve on these teams will get practice using problem-solving tools and will begin to develop some comfort in recommending actions. And third, we might start eliminating problems, which will begin to tamp down some of the fires we are dealing with." Danielle agreed and Jim filled in the words above the third post.

He took a picture of the chart with his phone to capture what they had discussed (Figure 4.2).

The next day, Jim met with Susan and the director of Human Resources. Susan brought with her a sealed envelope and Jim rightly assumed that her letter of resignation was contained within.

"Before you give me that envelope," Jim began. "I just wanted to start this meeting with an apology. It is clear to me that I got off on the wrong foot with my leadership team and began pushing my agenda without first taking the time to listen and respecting what you all have gone through with your past several bosses. For that, I am truly sorry. I know you have been frustrated with my leadership style. Last night, my wife was able to help me see that maybe I was asking for too big of a leap from where we are now and where I hope we will get to someday."

"Your wife sounds wise," replied Susan.

"This organization needs you Susan," said Jim. "And I could really use your help. It is clear to me that you are a hard worker, the employees respect you, and you ultimately want this organization to be the best it can be. I am not sure why the company executives went to the outside to fill the V.P. role, but I have got to assume that you were one of their top internal candidates. If you decide to stay, I promise to you that we will make this journey toward achieving excellence together one step at a time. I don't

FIGURE 4.2
Defining 4 Leadership Styles.

want to put pressure on you to stay, so I will accept your resignation letter if that is your final decision. But before you hand that to me, I wanted you to know where I stood."

Susan put her hand on the envelope to slide it across the table. She paused for just a moment to think about Jim's words. "Is there really something I could learn from this naïve, inexperienced, messed up boss?" she thought to herself.

THE STORY OF FRANK SMITH

Meanwhile, in the other division of JED, Inc., Frank Smith was deep in thought as he studied a spreadsheet in his office. "What numbers can I manipulate to make my metrics look just a little bit better?" he thought. Just when an idea began to form in his mind that Frank knew was going to be brilliant, a knocking sound at his office door rudely interrupted his thoughts.

"Excuse me, Mr. Smith," said a man in dirty coveralls standing just outside Frank's office. "My name is Scott. Do you have a minute? I could really use your help with a problem I am having."

"How did you get past my administrative assistant?" asked Frank with a great deal of irritation in his voice. "Oh, that's right… she had a doctor's appointment this afternoon. I guess this is my own fault since I was the one who forgot to close my office door. Well, since you already so rudely interrupted me, what do you want and please make it quick, I have a lot on my plate."

"Well, I have a bit of a safety concern at my machine," stammered the man. "We started using a new supplier a few weeks ago and the material they are sending us has a lot of problems. When I try to run this junk through my machine, the parts that are produced get stuck and the machine jams and shuts down. By the time I turn everything off, remove the safety guards, and get the parts unstuck, a lot of time goes by. My supervisor keeps yelling at me for not making my production numbers and is threatening to have me fired. I really need this job. Can you help?"

"Look, normally I would throw you out of my office for wasting my time on your little, insignificant problem," said Frank with a scowl. "But, since you said this was a safety issue, I guess legally, I need to respond. You go on back to your machine and I will see what I can do."

"Thank you so much, Mr. Smith. You have a good rest of your day," said Scott as he turned around to leave.

"Yeah... whatever," said Frank. He picked up his phone to call the director of purchasing. "Hey, I just had some bozo employee in my office complaining about material you bought. He says it is jamming his machine and he can't meet his production goals. Do you know what he is talking about?" After a short pause Frank replied, "Yes, that is a lot of savings on price. I can see now why you approved the change in suppliers. No, I don't want to give up those savings; our costs are already too high. We will never achieve excellence if we don't keep looking for ways to cut our costs. I will talk to the maintenance people... maybe they can give this machine operator a stick or something to help him unjam the parts and keep the machine going."

Later that day, Scott was working at his machine.

Ka-chunk... Ka-chunk... Ka-chunk.

There was a nice rhythm to the sound the machine made when it was running smoothly.

Ka-chunk... Ka-chunk... Ka –

Scott looked up and quickly realized that the machine had jammed again. "Dang, this is so frustrating," he thought. An hour ago, his supervisor had given him what looked like a sawed-off broom handle and told him to use it to unjam the parts. He also threatened, "If you ever go to the top brass without talking to me first, I will personally make sure you never step foot into this building ever again! The only reason I don't throw you out of this place right now is because you labeled your problem as a safety issue. The next time you go over my head, I don't care what the problem is, I swear, you will be terminated. Do I make myself perfectly clear!?!"

Scott had nodded his head and his supervisor left mumbling something about Scott's mother. "I am pretty sure he has never met my mother," Scott thought at the time. He grabbed the broom handle and began to try and unjam the part. No matter how far he reached, he could not quite get enough leverage to move the part. "Maybe, if I climb up one of the legs of the machine, I can get into a better position to pop that sucker off." Scott climbed up and reached over the safety guard with his stick. His entire arm was now well within the confines of the machine when to his horror the part popped off and the machine began to move.

Ka-Chunk.

PRACTICAL APPLICATIONS

What is the difference between a manager and a leader? I have asked this question in several of my workshops and the answers are fairly consistent. The word "manage" can be related to words such as control, status quo, stability, and in some cases, fear (Frank Smith). When people discuss the word "lead," they talk about movement, teamwork, accomplishments, mentoring, improvement, and even humility (Jim Brown).

A manager is usually connected with hierarchical organizational structures and the building of empires. Conventional thinking is that the more people you manage in your fiefdom, the better the chance you will be noticed for future promotions. Overseeing and controlling large groups of people requires a great deal of time and activity. One measure of how important a manager has become is the number of meetings that are double booked, the number of problems the person is juggling, and the hundreds of e-mails that are received on a daily basis. This leaves little time for developing visions and strategies and coaching people.

Leaders, on the other hand, tend to focus more of their time helping everyone in the organization move toward an inspirational vision of the future. This requires making it a priority to provide coaching, mentoring, training, and advising in order to get everyone on the same page and moving in the same direction. A good leader will give the credit to the employees when things go well and take the blame while seeking a better path forward when things go poorly.

There is a significant problem leaders run into when being compared with managers as far as promotions are concerned. As was stated earlier, managers look busy fighting fires and seem, from an outside perspective, as if they are making all of the hard decisions. Executives, CEOs, and board members may reward this behavior with pay raises, bonuses, and promotions. However, as a manager moves higher into the organizational structure, their ability to exert their control over all aspects of what is happening becomes more difficult. Many times throughout my career, I have witnessed managers who get big promotions and then fail miserably when their span of control becomes too great.

On the other hand, a good leader is also extremely busy but does most of the work behind the scenes. Once empowered teams of employees are up and running, the leader will have the opportunity to focus more of their time on interacting with customers, developing and getting buy-in for inspirational strategic visions of where the organization is going, assigning resources to help improve processes, and doing whatever is necessary to keep the organization moving forward. From the outside, it may appear that a successful leader isn't quite as frazzled and in control as a manager. Key metrics will all be moving in the right direction, employee morale will improve, and customers will be happier, but the leader may be overlooked as the teams seem to be making the improvements happen. In my opinion, this is one of the greatest reasons why managers (especially middle managers) resist improvement efforts that utilize teams of employees that require them to shift to being a leader: the fear of blending into the background and not being considered for future promotions. This is why there needs to be a new "normal" when defining an effective boss.

INTRODUCING THE LEADER PROGRESSION MODEL

What is effective leadership? How can it be defined? This is something that has been debated for many years. Throughout my career, I have witnessed many impactful leaders. However, the styles these leaders used seemed to vary significantly. Even the same leader might change the style they used depending on the current set of circumstances. This led to the creation of the leadership diagram Jim and his wife Danielle discuss in the story portion of this chapter that lists four different styles of leadership (Figure 4.3).

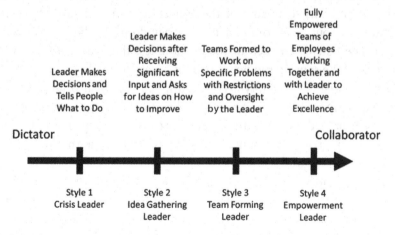

FIGURE 4.3
Leader Progression Model.

Style 1 – Leader Makes Decisions and Tells People What to Do: I like to think of this style as the "Crisis Leader." When an organization is enduring challenging circumstances, it will want someone who can step up and take charge and make the tough decisions in order to set things back onto a path of healing and growth. The analogy I like to use is: imagine if you were in a building that caught fire. The room is quickly filling with smoke and people are beginning to panic. Everyone would hope (and pray) that someone will step up, take charge, and begin barking out instructions in order to lead everyone to safety. This would not be a time for a committee to form, debate what to do, reach some sort of agreement, and then take action. More than likely, this would take a significant amount of time to complete and it would be too late to get everyone to safety (note that this approach might work if the group already had experience solving problems quickly – see "Style 4 Leadership").

Think about the character traits of a successful Crisis Leader. They would need to be able to assess a situation quickly, match that with previous knowledge and understanding about the enterprise, make a decisive decision, and have enough charisma, trust, and authority to get everybody to follow their lead. If all of these things are not part of the Crisis Leader's character, then disaster could happen. In the example of the room filling with smoke, what would happen if someone took charge and incorrectly decided that the situation was not all that bad and told everyone to stay in place? Or, what would happen if this person did not know the building layout and they ordered the group to vacate the room using the wrong escape route that ends in a dead end? What would happen if the leader hesitated and was so unsure of themselves that they could not reach a conclusion about what to do, or maybe they do make the right decision but no one listens? In each of these examples, the end result would be disastrous. The same could be said about an organizational situation. An impactful Crisis Leader (Style 1) would know the organization well, be able to quickly analyze any situation, make a final influential decision, and have the trust and respect of the employees to quickly implement the plan. This would increase the chance of a successful outcome that would lead them out of the crisis.

Style 2 – Leader Makes Decisions after Receiving Significant Input and Asks for Ideas on How to Improve: Once the crisis is in the rearview mirror, the leader can begin the process of moving the organization toward collaboration and teamwork. As has been pointed out in the story, many people, especially in middle management, will resist this change in leadership style. When people have worked for a dictator for a long period of time (especially if the leader stays in Crisis Leadership mode far past the end of the crisis), they grow complacent and become fearful of taking on the responsibility of making decisions. For example, in one organization, the person in charge used the dictator style for several years. When he left, the new boss began asking people to make their own decisions. Over half of the staff resigned within the first month. One of the staff, the director of human resources, said in her exit interview that she had accepted the position hoping that she would never need to make any significant decisions or take on any responsibility. She had hoped to work for someone who would tell her what to do and how to do it for the duration of her entire career.

How does a leader gently break the organization out of the habit of relying on the boss to make all of the decisions? Once the crisis is nearing an end, the leader will need to begin transitioning from Style 1 "Crisis Leader" to Style 2, the "Idea Gathering Leader." This leadership style depends on asking people for their inputs and ideas before a final decision is made. The person in charge will ask questions, listen intently to inputs from several sources, and then decide on a course of action.

One of the concerns of Style 2 leadership is that this is fairly easy to fake. In other words, the leader may have already made up their mind on what to do and just go through the motions of asking for input. If there is a lack of trust between the boss and the employees, there could be a perception that the leader is not being sincere when asking for ideas.

Why is the Idea Gathering Leader style critical to helping the organization move toward collaboration? By asking for people's input and ideas, it will initiate the development of critical thinking skills within the workforce. They will begin to see their work in a different light. "How can my process be better?" or "How would I do things differently?" will become part of a daily habit of looking for a better way to do things. When an employee, at any level, lifts up an idea or provides input to solving a problem, it is critically important that the leaders respond in a positive way. If it makes sense, has the potential of having a constructive impact by moving the organization closer to its vision, and there are resources available, the leader will begin building goodwill by finding a way to implement the employee's idea. If any (or all) of these criteria are not met, it will be important to thank the person and explain why this particular idea will not work at the present time. Then, ask for more ideas.

One way to facilitate this is to put a flip chart in the area where the leader would like to begin soliciting inputs for improvement and explain that as employees think of better ways to do their work, they should write the idea down (or tell their supervisor and they can do the writing) along with a date and their name. Once an idea is written, the only way it can be crossed off of the list is if the idea was implemented or the employee was given a good explanation as to why it cannot be done currently. One of the rules of this process is that the only person who can strike off an item on the list is the employee who came up with the idea. This becomes a great visual tool to see how many ideas are being gathered and how many have been addressed. It will be important to periodically celebrate, with the entire department, the ideas that do get implemented and to connect the improvements made to the overall performance of the organization. This will begin the process of building a sense of pride and accomplishment within the workers' ranks.

Asking for inputs and ideas is considered a step toward collaboration but it is not a huge leap since the leader is still taking responsibility for making the final decision. This allows the development of critical thinking skills without forcing people to be held accountable. Fear of failure can be difficult to overcome. However, when they see the leader make a decision to implement an idea, especially one that does not work, they will begin to overcome this fear. When failure does occur, it is important to figure out what went wrong and immediately start asking for new ideas to keep progress moving. This is the idea behind the Plan, Do, Check (or Study), Act cycle of improvement.

Style 3 – Teams Formed to Work on Specific Problems with Restrictions and Oversight by the Leader: Style 3, the "Team Forming Leader," begins when the first true problem-solving team is formed. Not only are the employees in this group sharing their ideas, but they are now being asked to make a recommendation for action. This will expand the critical thinking phase to now include taking on some responsibility for making a decision. The team's recommendation will still be vetted and approved by the leader, so the team is not 100% responsible. However, the "Team Forming Leader" will want to make sure that the team has the knowledge (data), tools, and methodology to make a recommendation that has a high probability of being accepted and ultimately working. There is a great thrill achieved within the team the first time it gets to participate in having one of its ideas implemented, and then witnesses the positive impact on the process. This continues to build a sense of pride and ownership that will continue to connect the employees with the success of the enterprise.

This is also an easy leadership style to fake. I have been a part of several teams that were asked to work on a specific problem or make an improvement happen and then find out later that it was all a façade and that the leaders had no intention of following up on any of the suggestions. If this happens, the leaders might as well go back to "old style" manager mode.

Style 4 – Fully Empowered Teams of Employees Working Together and with the Leader to Achieve Excellence: The word empowerment is thrown around quite a bit in organizations that are trying to change their culture. The "Empowerment Leader'" knows that this is one of the most difficult styles to successfully implement. Keep in mind that the leader is still in charge and responsible for the overall success of the organization. Empowerment does not mean anarchy. In order to reach this level of performance, the employees will need to have mastered the previous three styles and be ready to take on this new level of responsibility. This can easily take several years of training, practice, and research to accomplish. The types of decisions the team would be asked to make are also limited (this may expand over time). The first area of empowerment usually deals with the day-to-day decisions that will make sure the customer's needs are being met. Next, would be quick, on-the-spot problem solving to put out any fires that may occur (this would then need to trigger the use of a problem-solving team to try and figure out how to keep the problem from happening again). Some organizations have gone as far as allowing their teams to participate in the hiring process, provide input into the reward and recognition reviews, and decide how to launch new products or services in their part of the business. I would argue that an organization that has achieved Style 4 leadership throughout the enterprise will be close to (or even surpass) achieving what the Japanese implemented decades ago.

Two final points to make about the Leadership Progression Model (Figure 4.3): first, this model is meant to be fluid. In other words, a good leader may need to move back and forth, using different leadership styles depending on the current situation. For example, if a leader has gotten the entire organization to Style 3 or 4 and a new crisis occurs, then there may be a need to revert back to Style 1 to deal with the current situation. This will need to be explained to the organization so the employees do not become frustrated (most people I have worked with say that once they experience what it is like to work as a team, they do not want to go back to the old ways). The second point is that various parts of the organization may move along this progression at different speeds. You may have one leader who grasps this new way of thinking and quickly moves their group to Style 3 while everyone else is still trying to figure out how to make Style 2 work. In one organization, the CEO actually uses this leadership diagram to keep track of which style each of their leaders is currently utilizing, at every level within the company. They then use the Leadership Progression Model as a way to have discussions on what it would take to move that part of the organization to the next style.

We will be exploring each of the different leadership styles in more depth throughout the rest of this book.

5

Style One Leadership –
The Crisis Leader

*What is the difference between "old style" management
and a crisis leader (Style 1)?*

THE STORY OF FRANK SMITH

"What is all of the commotion out there!?!" yelled Frank. "I am trying to get important work done and can't hear myself think!"

"Something is going on in the factory," responded his administrative assistant. "I think a worker might have gotten hurt."

"Dang it! This is going to impact my safety numbers and may put our efforts to achieve excellence in jeopardy. I better go out and see what is going on." Frank grabbed his safety gear and headed toward the entrance to the factory. He followed the crowd to an area that contained large machines stamping out parts. "Hmm… This is the department where that dirty, little fellow who bothered me earlier today works," thought Frank. He saw a large group of people standing around what looked like a man lying on the ground. "All right! All right! Everybody back to work!" shouted Frank as he pushed his way through the crowd. "I am in charge now and will take care of everything. There is nothing to see here! Get back to work and don't miss your production goals!" Frank saw Bill, the director of quality, helping the man on the floor sit up.

"What happened?" asked Scott as he began checking his arms and legs for any cuts or broken bones.

"You came close to losing your arm and maybe your life," replied Bill. "I was walking by your workstation when I saw you up on your machine trying to pry a part out using some sort of stick. I walked over to tell you to get down and then noticed the machine winding up to make the next part. I grabbed your belt and yanked with all of my strength just as the jaws of the machine slammed shut. We both fell backward and you must have hit your head on the ground and blacked out for a moment. Where did you get the foolish idea to bypass the safety guards by using a stick to unjam your machine?"

"We don't need to get into all of that right now," interrupted Frank before Scott could respond. "All that I care about is that our worker here is safe and has no lasting injuries. How are you feeling?"

"I think I will be okay," said Scott. "I guess we will need to write this up in the safety log. I hate to be the one who ruins our perfect safe workplace streak."

"Well, you look like you are going to bounce back with no problems. I tell you what," said Frank, "how about taking the rest of the day off to fully recover and let's just call this a 'near miss?' That way our safety metrics will stay intact and we will still be on a good road toward achieving excellence."

Scott thanked Bill for his help and Frank for giving him some time off. He then gathered his personal effects and headed home. Frank called over Scott's supervisor to discuss the situation. "I can't believe you allowed this to happen!" yelled Frank. "Next time, we might not be so lucky. Log Scott's absence as 'personal time' so our productivity metrics are not negatively impacted and I expect you to run his machine to make sure we do not miss our production numbers!"

"What about the parts jamming issue?" asked the supervisor.

"Tell the maintenance folks to design a better stick to unjam the parts so this does not happen again!" yelled Frank over his shoulder as he headed back to his office. "I am the only one around here who seems to care about this business," he muttered to himself. "Another fire successfully put out by me."

When he got back to his desk, the operations manager was waiting for him. "I heard about Scott and am glad that he is going to be okay," he told Frank. "We're dealing with several major quality and production issues today. I am not sure if we are going to make our numbers with all of these problems. It just seems that some days we are so snake-bitten and unlucky."

"Look," said Frank. "You need to be tougher with the workers. Tell them to try a little harder. Make sure they know that their job is on the line if they do not perform and achieve good quality and make their production goals."

"The workers don't have control over the bad material we are buying or the fact that their machines keep breaking down because we slashed our maintenance budgets," replied the head of operations.

"Those are just excuses," replied Frank. "Every organization has problems to overcome. That is why we pay you and the rest of the staff. I am getting tired of being the only one around here with all the answers. If we do not show significant progress toward achieving excellence, then I will find a new batch of managers who will get the job done. Do you understand?"

As the operations manager left shaking his head and mumbling something about the need to turn their luck around, Frank sat down at his desk and let out a long sigh and thought, "this place would so fall apart if it was not for me holding it all together. I hope my boss realizes how important I am to keeping things under control around here. I should be nominated for the manager of the year award."

THE STORY OF JIM BROWN

A few days later, Frank's counterpart, Jim Brown, was about to start his weekly staff meeting. Everyone filed into the conference room and looked at the empty chair where Susan Jones normally sat. The group was especially quiet and it felt like a funeral was about to begin. "Well, I was hoping that after taking a couple of days off to think about things, Susan would change her mind about leaving," thought Jim. "I guess we will need to start looking for a new director of operations."

"Sorry I am late," said Susan as she entered the conference room to the great relief of everyone in attendance. "I got held up in traffic. It is good to be back and I look forward to working with each of you to help us get on a path toward making improvement happen." She looked up at Jim and said, "So, what did I miss and what is the plan for moving forward, boss?"

"Glad to have you back," said Jim. "Let's get to work and as a team, see how much improvement can be realized. During the past several days, I have been analyzing mounds of data. For the first time in a long while, we are getting real, true information about our performance, and it is not painting a good picture. We have many holes to address to keep this ship from sinking. To begin, I want us all to focus on two priorities over the next couple of months: safety and cleanliness."

"I thought our safety numbers were pretty good," said the director of finance. "We have had only three minor accidents so far this year and none of them resulted in any lost time. Don't we have bigger fish to fry in other areas of the business such as our costs and quality?"

"I took a look at the three investigation reports," replied Jim. "And we got extremely lucky that those accidents did not result in serious injury or even death. If a couple of things had gone slightly differently, we would be in deep trouble with our safety numbers and several of our employees, who trust us to provide a safe work environment, may have ended up in a hospital or worse. I have asked the supervisors to begin logging what are called 'near misses' and 'proactive audit failures.' These are safety concerns that do not result in an official accident report but could turn into a real problem if not quickly addressed. It is critically important that every employee understands that we are going to do everything possible to keep them safe or we will never gain the trust of all of our workers. I want each of you to begin doing daily safety walks throughout the factory, office area, and customer service center looking for any unsafe practice or condition that might injure an employee."

"What!?!" exclaimed Linda, the director of purchasing. "I don't have time to do safety audits."

"You mean you don't know how to do a safety audit," said David, the director of facilities.

"I want each of you to spend one hour a day helping us improve our safety," said Jim. "Don't worry, we will provide training to make sure everyone knows what to look for and how to record any concerns. The maintenance folks are committed to helping address any issues we are able to uncover. It has been demonstrated in other companies that the more safety defects that can be proactively fixed, the risk of injuries will drop. I have visited other organizations that have been able to achieve near-flawless safety performances for multiple years. We owe it to our employees to focus on achieving this level of excellence so families do not worry if their loved ones will be coming home at the end of their shift."

"Boss, I am going to need an exemption from doing these safety walks," said the director of marketing. "We have a big show coming up soon and it will be important that we do a good job of showcasing our new products."

"Don't you have a solid group of folks who will be putting this show together and isn't it pretty much the same as what you did last year and the year before?" asked Jim. "I think you can afford one hour a day to help with these audits. This is not optional. It is important that every one of our employees sees their entire leadership team make this an ultra-high priority. If the corporate people complain about you not being able to make all of the meetings to prepare for this show, tell them to give me a call. I will make sure you get the cover you need to help us achieve this first step toward getting this place back on track."

"You also mentioned cleanliness," said the director of finance. "What is that all about?"

"I would like everyone to put on your safety glasses and follow David, our facilities director, to the back of the factory," said Jim. "He has been working on something that I think you all need to see."

The staff got up and followed David as he led the group through a maze of machines and pallets of parts. "I think this is the first time some of you have ventured out to where we make our products," said Jim. "If you have any questions about how to navigate around these large machining centers in a safe manner, please do not hesitate to ask." They approached an opening that led to a small room that contained one of the production work groups that assembled part of the products they produced. There was a large tarp covering the entrance that prevented the group from seeing the room on the other side. David was visibly animated as he stood next to the entrance and grabbed the tarp in order to pull it down at the appropriate time.

"A clean and organized workspace goes hand-in-hand with a safe workspace," said Jim. "Our factory, office space, and customer service centers are embarrassing as far as how dirty and unorganized everything seems to be. I would never want to purposefully bring a customer into this environment. I mean, look around you. Notice how dark and dirty everything is? There is oil on the floor, trash in the aisles, parts stacked everywhere with no rhyme or reason as to where anything goes. The floor and ceiling have turned black from years of grime build up. And look at the walls in here as well as the office space. Who thought that 'battleship gray' was a good color to paint everything? Notice how many windows are cracked or boarded up? It feels like everyone is working in a dark, dank, dirty dungeon. Who can feel a sense of pride and excitement coming to work in such awful conditions?"

"What are you proposing?" asked Linda. "Do you want us to grab some mops and clean the floor when we are doing the safety walks?" Her voice was dripping with sarcasm.

"No," laughed Jim. "This is going to take much more than a simple mop to address. And don't worry, Linda, this is something I have asked

Susan and David to address. In fact, David and the facilities folks have already been at work on this request. They solicited inputs from Susan's production workers and focused on making the room behind this tarp a model of what I would like to see happen in our entire workspace." With that said, Jim turned to David and gave him a nod. David pulled a rope and the tarp came crashing down revealing the room behind.

"Woah!" exclaimed the group in unison as they saw the room behind the tarp. The place was bright and clean and well organized. The floor had been painted a bright gray with a tough epoxy coating and the walls and ceiling had been cleaned and painted white in order to reflect the light and make the room gleam. "We installed super-bright, energy-efficient lights so the workers can see what they are doing," said David. "We also put in several work benches, shelving units, and cabinets in order to store stuff and get things off of the floor. Everything is labeled and the workers have agreed to help keep all of this in place."

When David mentioned the workers, Jim's staff looked at the faces of the employees working in this new, polished room and could not help but notice the huge grins on everyone's face. Even Susan was visibly impressed with the transformation. "Wow, David! You and your folks, along with the production workers, did a super nice job cleaning and organizing this place. I can see how this would have a positive impact on our employees. We will need to make sure we give them the tools and time to keep it this way. I have already picked out the next workspace to upgrade."

"How much is all of this going to cost?" asked the director of finance. "What is the return on this investment? I mean, we have a business to run here. I think it is great that our employees might feel better about where they work, but will that make them more productive? Is our quality going to improve? I doubt clean floors and walls will make that much of a difference."

"We are going to save a ton in energy costs with these new lights," said David. "Not enough to offset the total costs of doing this, but it is a start."

"There are also a lot of intangibles that might not hit the bottom line of our financial report but are still important to consider," said Jim. "When things go wrong around here, employees say that we had 'bad luck.' I want us to build a system of processes that are so robust and predictable, that luck is no longer part of our vocabulary. With a clean work environment, it will be easier to see leaks form that might cause people to slip and fall resulting in injury. Also, if a leak does form, that will be an indicator that something is wrong such as a machine that is about to run out of oil or a pipe that is about to burst. As we get the place more organized, it will be easier to locate parts and supplies and also allow us to put in a system to make sure we don't run out of what we need. This will ultimately lead to a smoother running operation and reduce the risk of missing shipments. We have many more steps to complete before seeing real improvements, but having a clean, safe, bright work environment will become the foundation we will need to build on in order to achieve excellence. My hope is that one day, we will be proud to invite our customers in to show them that we are serious about meeting their needs."

It was clear the director of finance was not sold. "Well," said Jim. "You all wanted a boss who tells you what to do. Consider this a mandate and I will take all of the responsibility for this decision if anyone at corporate complains."

Later that day, Jim met with Susan in the company cafeteria for a cup of coffee. "I am glad you decided to stay," said Jim. "I think we are starting to develop a plan to move this massive ship in a new direction and I would like your help to take us to the next step on our journey."

"I don't know," said Susan. "I am still trying to wrap my head around this decision to stay. Please don't make me regret tearing up that resignation letter."

"Don't worry. This is a simple but critically important request. I would like you to pick a few employees and begin asking them to share any ideas they might have on ways we can improve what we do around here. Try to select employees in several different departments and be sure to ask a few of the factory workers to participate as well. Also, be sure to include some supervisors and middle managers."

"That sounds like more than 'just a few employees,'" said Susan. "Do you want this done in a big group and what do you want me to do with all of these ideas?"

"No, actually, I would prefer that you do this one-on-one to get started. Later on we can start using groups of people. Some of our employees may not be ready yet to share their inputs in front of their peers. It would be great if you could write up their ideas on big pieces of paper and tape them up on the walls of our main entrance. I would like every employee to see this collection of thoughts as they enter each morning and hopefully that will begin to encourage all of our workers to think of their own improvement ideas as well. We will need all of this input and every worker to get involved if we want to truly achieve a new level of excellence. I appreciate your help on this and let me know if there is anything I can do to assist."

That evening, Jim was about to pack up his briefcase and head home when his phone rang. He could see from the display that it was his boss calling. "Hello, Jim Brown speaking... Oh, hey boss. Yes, I did see the latest quality and safety numbers for this business. I know that both numbers took a huge step in the wrong direction. Remember though, we discussed this. These new numbers reflect what is really going on around here. For many years, defects and safety problems were hidden and the reports were not at all accurate. We will never get better if we are not honest with ourselves as far as how bad things really are. Yes... Yes but... No, I am not satisfied with these numbers. That is the point. None of us should be happy with this horrible level of performance. Keep in mind that this is the way things have always been, we are just shining a light on the problem. Yes, sir... I understand that the top brass is not happy... Yes, I do have a plan. Please be patient as we get the holes patched in this massive ship. I understand... you will run out of patience pretty fast if you don't see substantial results. You have my word that the results will be forthcoming. Goodnight to you too, sir." Jim hung up the phone. "I sure hope we can pull this off," he thought with a sigh as he turned out the lights and headed home.

PRACTICAL APPLICATIONS

The story portion of this chapter begins to expose the differences between a manager (Frank) and a leader (Jim). Even Style 1 leadership, "the Crisis Leader," which is on the dictator side of the leadership progression, is far removed from the typical manager. One of the most obvious differences is demonstrated when a problem occurs. An old style manager will want to take control of the situation and then determine a path that will have the least amount of negative impact and get things back to the way they were before the crisis. Common statements such as "This is how we are going to dig ourselves out of this hole" or "Let's go into damage control mode and contain the situation" indicate a desire to push through the problem and to control the narrative as much as possible. Managers tend to want to put the best light possible on a bad situation and if all else fails, figure out who to blame for the crisis. Once the problem is contained, then the manager will want to quickly move on to the next problem (and blame all of these reoccurring issues on bad luck).

The Style 1 leader, on the other hand, has a longer view of a particular situation. They will want to also address the current crisis with some stop-gap measures but in addition will want to figure out a way to keep the problem from reoccurring by changing and improving the process. They will want to use this opportunity to help the organization learn how to work as a team to address the crisis in order to move toward the collaborative side of the leadership diagram. Crisis leaders will ask questions such as "What can we learn from this problem?", "What did we do well as a team when confronted with a difficult situation and what could we have done better?", and "What do we need to change in the process or system to keep this from ever happening again?" The goal of a Crisis Leader is to come out on the other side of a problem with a stronger set of processes and a more knowledgeable team who are better prepared to handle the next situation. A Crisis Leader will even praise the group for uncovering the problem, bringing it to the leader's attention, and assisting with the solution. When this is the approach a leader takes when a crisis occurs, fear of sharing bad information and fear of failure begins to evaporate throughout the organization.

Another way to see the difference between a manager and a Style 1 – "Crisis Leader" is to watch how they deal with data. Managers tend to want to do whatever is necessary to keep data from looking bad or moving in the wrong direction. Some might view bad data as a sign of weakness that could prevent a manager from getting the next promotion or pay raise. A Crisis Leader, on the other hand, will want the data to be as accurate and visible as possible, even if this paints a bad picture of the situation. They will then dig into the data and use the information to help uncover the root of the problem in order to permanently fix the situation.

The Style 1 leader knows that the only way to instigate improvement is to get the entire organization to admit that there is a need to change. One of the ways to make this a reality is by exposing unflattering data to the entire organization. One leader I worked with called this the "ugly" data and often spoke about the need to expose both the good data and the ugly data in order to determine what needed to be fixed and to establish a beginning point so improvement progress could be accurately measured.

As a way to demonstrate the difference between managers and leaders when it comes to the use of data, the following example might help shed some light. In a fairly large, global corporation, the two dozen business units would report how they were performing on a monthly basis. It was clear that, in many instances, what was being reported was not accurate to what was actually happening within these business units. The CEO determined that there would be "a day of amnesty" when it came to reporting safety, quality, and customer satisfaction data. This would allow these businesses to clean up their data and begin reporting what was actually happening without any form of retribution. About half of the business units decided to submit the same numbers they had always reported, refusing to admit that they were not doing as well as the data indicated (after a bit of investigating it was fairly easy to determine that the data painted a far better picture than what was actually happening). Managers within these businesses were trying to control the narrative and spin the data to make things appear better than they really were. The other half of the business units took the opportunity to reevaluate their data and determined that the numbers were not reflective of what was actually happening. They eventually reported results that were far worse than was previously believed (but were closer to reality). The CEO, to his credit, did not unleash his fury on these businesses but instead praised them for their honesty and committed financial resources to help them with their improvement efforts. These organizations had Style 1 leaders who were willing to admit that they had problems and needed to go into crisis mode. It did not take long for these businesses to begin showing significant improvement.

ACTIONS OF A STYLE 1 LEADER

The Crisis Leader may seem like an old style manager when they step in and start making decisions. However, they also recognize a need to begin the process of getting buy-in and commitment from the employees. To show Style 1 leadership in action, in the story portion of this chapter, Jim explained the seriousness of the safety data and that the three accidents could have been much worse if things had gone slightly differently. In other words, because of good luck, three employees did not suffer significant injury or death. Leaders do not believe in good or bad luck... only good or bad processes. Jim made a decision and dictated that everyone would participate in safety walks and audits. He also clarified why it was important for everyone to participate (the need to provide a safe work environment, build trust with the employees, and show a united leadership team who considered this a top priority) and had already thought about the need to provide training and assistance in order to not embarrass any of his staff who might not have experience in this area. Jim explained that he would personally take responsibility for any missed assignments and that he would provide cover for all of the staff members. These are all things a Crisis Leader would do in order to win the support and trust of their employees.

In another example, Jim could have mandated that all of the factory and office spaces be cleaned, organized, painted, etc. or else something bad would happen. Instead, he had the director of facilities, along with a group of production workers, clean and organize one small portion of the factory in order to show his staff (and the rest of the workers) what was possible and the difference this change would make to the morale of the employees and the well-being of the process. By taking this route, he was able to get some (not all) of his staff on board. Having the buy-in of the employees, supervisors, and staff will allow the implementation of improvements to go faster and smoother and have a far greater chance of long-term sustainability. A great idea with little to no buy-in will have a far greater chance of failure than a good idea that has significant support and buy-in.

In addition to getting out of the current situation, the Crisis Leader knows that the only way to achieve sustainable, long-term levels of excellent performance is to help the entire organization grow in its ability to quickly respond to problems and continuously look for ways to improve how things get done. The progression of the leader through the four different styles discussed in the last chapter allows the employees to learn and develop a culture of teamwork, customer focus, and continuous improvement.

Figure 5.1 shows the natural progression that is realized when the leader migrates from Style 1 to Style 4. For example, if a Style 1 – Crisis Leader is able to convey the seriousness of the current situation, make quick and conclusive decisions, and is able to rally the employees around specific fixes, the organization will learn how to implement rapid and decisive actions in order to quickly put out the fires that are causing the crisis. When a Style 2 – Idea Gathering Leader begins to ask employees for ideas on ways to make things better, the organization is learning to think about the work they are doing and question the way their processes function. This improves their critical thinking skills and begins to develop a process

Organizational Progression	Style 1 Crisis Leader	Style 2 Idea Gathering Leader	Style 3 Team Forming Leader	Style 4 Empowerment Leader
Rapid & Decisive Actions	✓	✓	✓	✓
Critical Thinking & Process Improvement		✓	✓	✓
Problem Analysis & Solution Recommendations			✓	✓
Customer Responsiveness & Pride of Work				✓

FIGURE 5.1

Organizational Progression.

improvement culture. When a Style 3 – Team Forming Leader asks a group of employees to come together to solve a problem, they will be introduced to tools that will allow the team to analyze data in order to get to the root cause of a problem. They will also be asked to recommend a course of action. This will help the team focus on reaching consensus on a possible solution to the problem without the fear of being held accountable if the solution does not work (the leader still makes the final decision). And Style 4 – the Empowerment Leader helps the teams of employees develop an understanding of customers' needs (both internal and external) and respond quickly to changes and problems. This leads to great ownership and pride in the overall success of the organization.

One additional note about the difference between a manager and a Style 1 leader: since leadership is associated with change and improvement versus keeping things the same, it takes a great deal of courage to be an effective leader. Jim knew that it would be controversial to tear up the old quality reports and begin reporting the real data in order to build a case for change and improvement. This is especially brave considering the fact that the executives of JED, Inc. are clearly not supportive of such a move. Maybe they are afraid that this bad data will leak out to the customer base or taint their standing with their investors. However, without this honest look at the real data, the chance of achieving excellence is greatly diminished.

To highlight this point, I had the opportunity to work with an extremely brave leader at one point in my career. This person was hired to run a business that had done pretty well for several decades. The product that was being produced was well respected by the customer base, the profit margins were strong, and the business enjoyed a healthy market share (a strong #1 position). When this person was hired into the top position, he was told to focus on managing everything in order to keep things the way they were and to not "mess up" the business. However, after analyzing the data, this new leader decided there was much room to improve. He went down the same path being portrayed by Jim Brown in the story (use of empowered teams, engagement of all of the employees, getting everyone focused on working together to achieve a common vision, etc.). After three years of hard work, changing the culture and getting the organization to Style 4, the business experienced tremendous growth as customer satisfaction improved significantly. Profit margins increased dramatically as did the overall market share. This dramatic increase in performance for a business that was already considered to be doing well shocked the corporate executives. It took tremendous courage for this leader to challenge the status quo and make changes to a healthy business in order to get closer to achieving excellence.

6

Style Two Leadership – The Fact Gathering Leader

"Vision is not seeing things as they are, but as they will be"
– Fortune Cookie

THE STORY OF JIM BROWN

Jim Brown's director of operations was about to do something she had little experience ever doing, asking for help. Susan Jones's entire career had been centered on telling other people what to do or being told what to do. She was now about to ask a production worker for ideas on how to improve their own process and had to write the idea down and post the information for everyone to see. "I can't believe I am being asked to collect ideas from people who are so far down the chain of command," Susan thought as she began trying to find her first volunteer. "I doubt anyone will have much to contribute and those who do will probably have no idea what they are talking about." She noticed a middle-aged woman about to take a break from doing her work and walked over.

"Excuse me," said Susan. "Do you mind if I interrupt your break and ask you a couple of questions? My name is Susan Jones and I would like to discuss any ideas you might have in how we could get better."

"Yes, I know who you are Ms. Jones. My name is Mary Robinson and I have worked here for over 10 years and I believe that this is the first time someone in your position has spoken to me. Am I in some sort of trouble? Did I do something wrong? Oh my… am I being fired? I can't afford to lose this job!"

"No, Mary, your job is safe. As you probably know, we have a new V.P. running this business and he would like to shake things up a bit around here. He would like some of the workers to share ideas on ways we can improve our processes."

"Wait… Isn't that your job?" asked Mary. "Aren't you supposed to supply ideas on how to get better? I think this is all a way to get rid of jobs and then blame me and the other workers when things turn bad. Why should I trust you to do the right thing?"

"You know, Mary, I can see why you might feel this way. I guess we have not done a very good job of building trust with any of our workers."

"I am constantly being told by my supervisor to quit thinking and just do my job," replied Mary. "And if I don't meet my quotas or make a mistake of some kind, I am told that my rear end will be out on the street. Then, I get bad material to work with and a machine that is constantly breaking down… kind of hard to build trust when things are this bad for the workers."

"Look," said Susan with a tone of frustration, "I am sorry to interrupt your break. Please head back to work and forget this ever happened. I knew this was a bad idea." With that said, she put away her notebook and got up to leave.

Before Susan had gotten too far down the aisle, Mary shouted, "If I give you some ideas, what are you going to do with them? I mean, if I am going to go to all of the trouble to share with you how we can do things better, I deserve to know how these ideas are going to be used. Are you going to write them down in your notebook and then toss them into the trash? Or, use them as your own and try to get a promotion?"

Susan turned around and walked back to where Mary was sitting. "No, Mary… none of those things. Actually, I am going to write your ideas down, along with several others, on big pieces of paper and post them in the entrance of the building for everyone to see. If you would like, I can include your name for each of your ideas or you can be anonymous, whichever you prefer. Then, our goal will be to decide which ideas to implement. Once these decisions are made, you have my word that I will return and let you know what happened."

"Humph!" replied Mary. "I still don't trust you or your new boss. It was pretty cool though when he tore up those quality reports in the parking lot the other day. Most of us knew that those reports were not worth squat and had no reflection on what was really going on around here. I really do need this job and hope to work here for as long as I can… maybe things really will change. For 10 years, I have been performing work at this station and have had a lot of time to think about doing all of these tasks in a different way. For example, all of my parts are stored way over there on shelves by the aisle. Why can't they be stored here at my workstation? I must walk 5 miles a day just getting the parts I need to do my job."

Susan wrote Mary's idea down and then the flood gates opened. After 15 minutes, Susan had recorded over a dozen ideas on ways to improve this one workstation. She thanked Mary for her inputs and again promised to get back to her regarding what would happen. "Wow," thought Susan as she headed back to her office. "This was not what I was expecting. With no real training on how to improve processes, Mary was able to give me several good ways to make things run smoother. Maybe our workers actually do have something to contribute when it comes to deciding how we can get better."

Later that week, Susan and Jim Brown were standing in the entrance hall of the business looking at the 23 large pieces of paper taped to the walls that contained over a hundred ideas. "This is amazing," said Jim. "I was not expecting this much input in such a short period of time. Our employees at all levels must have been thinking about ways to make things better for quite some time."

"Yeah, I agree," said Susan. "I was impressed by most of the ideas. You can see that several of them are pretty easy fixes and make a lot of sense."

"Why do you think that the easy ones haven't already been implemented?" asked Jim.

"Well... this is embarrassing," stammered Susan, "but I think it all boils down to lack of communication and involvement. In other words, no one bothered to ask."

"I count 24 ideas that can, and should, be implemented right away," said Jim.

"I agree," said Susan. "I will get with David in the facilities group and we will start putting a plan together. That leaves over 90 ideas that will require some in-depth investigation and planning to sort through. We don't have the resources to dig through all of the analysis required to figure out which ideas to implement next. How are we going to prioritize this massive list?"

"Hmmm..." thought Jim out loud. "That is a very good question. I think what we are missing is a vision of where this business is going over the next couple of years. If we had that nailed down, then it would be easier to determine which ideas would help us achieve our vision and which ones would need to be moved to the back burner."

"Don't we have a company mission statement?" asked Susan. "Doesn't that determine our direction?"

"No, not really," replied Jim. "A mission statement explains why we exist… what the purpose of our organization is all about. The way I have used 'vision' in the past is to help define an inspirational picture of the future that will help focus the entire organization on achieving something greater than what it is experiencing now. The vision needs to be something tangible that everyone in the organization can connect with and rally around. Whereas the mission tends to be a single statement that looks good on business cards or on posters and does not change much from year to year, a vision is more fluid. I personally prefer using bullet points to describe various aspects of the vision."

"So, the vision is stuff like, 'we want to grow the business by a certain amount' or 'make a certain amount of money?' That sounds like goal setting to me," said Susan.

"No, actually a good vision does not include results. The focus instead is on what has changed that ultimately will lead to better results. Instead of saying something like, 'our vision is to double our profits,' we would use something like, 'our vision is, in two to three years, to have teams of empowered employees working together, using processes that are predictable and well thought out and to seamlessly launch at least one new service and one new product that will satisfy and exceed the needs and desires of our customers.' When we do all of these things well, this will lead to more sales and less cost per part, resulting in more profits. If we wanted to get more specific, we could have several bullet points that describe various details. For example, a specific detail might be to replicate and maintain a work environment throughout the building that looks like that small factory room David and his facilities team helped clean up and organize the other day."

"Do you, as our boss, develop this vision and tell us what you want?" asked Susan.

"No, actually, the way this works is to first get input from workers in all of the various departments, including sales and marketing to get our customers' perspectives, and then sit down as a leadership team and develop this vision together. Maybe that needs to be the next step on our journey. We need to go off-site for a couple of days and figure out what our future might look like. I know a good facilitator who can help us," said Jim. "We could also visit some other organizations that have already been on this journey to get some ideas of what excellence looks like."

"I have to agree that having a common vision of where we are heading would be beneficial," said Susan. "And, maybe it would help your staff come together more as a team if we were all pulling in the same direction."

"And, it would help us sort through all of these improvement ideas. I would like to make this happen as quickly as possible. Let the other staff members know that I will be asking for inputs on when we can go off-site for a couple of days. And, Susan thanks for your help in soliciting these ideas. This is really great work and a huge step toward achieving collaboration with our employees."

THE STORY OF FRANK SMITH

Meanwhile, Frank Smith's division was barely able to keep the wheels on. His group of managers was constantly putting out multiple fires that sprang up every day. The data continued to look great, but the reality was much different. Frank was in a particularly foul mood as he hung up the phone after speaking to his boss. He had been having a discussion with Bill, his director of quality about a slight increase in customer complaints when the phone had interrupted a perfectly good tirade Frank was spewing.

"Dang it!" said Frank to Bill. "That was my boss. Apparently, that new guy, Jim something or other, who is running our sister division on the other side of the state, has put some cockamamie ideas into his head. He asked the workers to provide ideas on how to get better! Can you believe that nonsense? What a waste of time!"

"That must be an indication that he is panicking and has no clue how to get his business on track," replied Bill.

"Yeah, you are probably right. Well, his incompetence has created a new problem for us. The boss wants us to do something similar. I am not going to waste my time getting ideas on how to improve. We are doing just fine without this kind of distraction."

"So, are you going to ignore your boss?" asked Bill.

"No, I am smarter than that," said Frank as he glared at his quality director. "Hmmm... What can I do to get the boss off of my back? I have an idea. We need to redesign our product brochure. I will personally pull together a group of our best employees and ask for their thoughts on what they would like to see with this new brochure. That way, I can honestly say I am getting inputs from others. Bill, I want you to set this meeting up and make sure everyone is there. You help me pull this off and maybe I won't dock your pay due to the customer complaints going up."

Later that week, Frank strolled into the conference room, 10 minutes late. Seated around the table were a dozen employees who were not quite sure why they had been asked to attend this meeting or even what the meeting was about. Only two of the attendees were from the marketing department and had any idea what a good brochure might look like. Frank began the meeting by passing out a mockup of something he had put together to get the ball rolling. "Just to be clear," Frank began, "I am seeking input on how to design the next version of our product marketing materials. The final decision will be mine to make. I think the material I just gave you will accomplish everything needed to educate our customers and get them to buy our products and services. Does anyone disagree?"

One of the marketing people raised her hand. "I have a few suggestions on how to make this brochure even better," she began. "For example, I would go with a different color scheme since all of our research shows that the colors in this mockup are those used in our competitor's logo and will make our customers think of them instead of us."

"Well," began Frank's rebuttal, "I disagree. Everyone knows the colors I picked out will have a positive impact on the perception of those who look at this marketing campaign. Any other, more useful ideas on how this can be done better?"

One of the production workers from the factory raised his hand. "I am not entirely sure why I am here since I don't have any experience in marketing stuff. However, I do know our products pretty well and the claims made on the back of the brochure about the performance do not match reality as far as our factory tests are concerned. Isn't that against the rules to make false claims like that?"

"Look," said Frank. "You are right when you say you don't know marketing stuff. I am not entirely sure why you are here wasting my time. It is a common practice in our industry to paint the products in the best possible light. Everyone does it. What you are looking at on the factory floor are average performance measurements. We can take the best product data and include that and correctly claim that at least some of our product performs this well."

"But you left out the word 'some,'" replied the factory worker. "Isn't that misleading?"

Frank's patience was already about to run out and the meeting was just getting started. "We do not have time to educate you on the ways marketing works. You will just have to trust me that this is the way things are done. Now, does anyone else have an intelligent idea to offer?"

There was a 30-second pause as everyone tried to decide if it was worth jeopardizing their career to speak up. Finally, the person from marketing who spoke first stood up and went to one of the whiteboards in the room. She began to quickly sketch an entirely different concept to how the brochure might look. As she was drawing, the rest of the group, with the exception of Frank, began to throw out comments and ideas. She acknowledged these inputs and incorporated them into her drawing. Frank tried to interrupt several times but was unable to overcome the enthusiasm that was building within the room. Forty minutes later, all of the whiteboards in the room were covered with new, fresh ways to display the products that would quickly grab the attention of anyone who looked at the brochure. When the person from marketing put down her pen, the entire room, with one exception, erupted in applause. Frank was seething.

"I appreciate your enthusiasm," he said through gritted teeth and a strained voice. "But this is not the right direction. However, I will take all of your inputs into consideration as we design the final marketing materials. Thank you for your inputs. Now, please get back to your workstations and I expect no decrease in productivity."

Later that week, Frank stopped by Bill's office. "We have ordered the marketing brochures. We can check the box that we got inputs from our workers and incorporated them into one of our projects. You are someone I can trust. I need you to get this invoice paid... and use discretion."

After Frank left, Bill wondered why Frank said to 'use discretion.' He then noticed the date on the invoice that showed when the brochures had been ordered. The date indicated that the brochures had been ordered 2 days before the employee input meeting Frank hosted. "That snake," thought Bill, "he had no intention of using anyone's inputs. Maybe he was afraid they would steal some of the credit."

PRACTICAL APPLICATIONS

The story portion of this chapter covers two key points. First, we are introduced to what a Style 2 – Idea Gathering Leader looks like in action. On the surface, it seems like it would be fairly easy to ask employees for their ideas on ways to improve their processes. However, if there is a lack of trust, which is usually the case when trying to change the culture, the employees may resist because they might think that there are nefarious reasons as to why they are being included. Second, Jim realizes that without a vision, it is difficult to sort the ideas on ways to improve. This introduces the concepts of Mission, Vision, Strategy, and Values. We will dive a bit deeper into both of these points.

STYLE 2 – THE IDEA GATHERING LEADER

As was discussed in the previous chapter, the Style 2 – Idea Gathering Leader's objective is to begin to stimulate the critical thinking of the employees by asking for their inputs and ideas. One way to do this is simply to ask questions such as, "Is there an improvement that would help you do your job?" or, "What would you suggest we do to get rid of wasted effort in this part of the process?" or, "Is there a specific change you would like to see made to the product or process that would help make the customer happier?" The point of these questions is to get the employees thinking about a positive change, something that will make their jobs better. Avoid asking questions such as "What is wrong with your process?" or "What do you not like about your job?" This leads down a path that could turn ugly.

However, the Style 2 leader knows that it is imperative to only ask these improvement idea gathering questions if there is a real desire to get this feedback. The employee will watch closely to see if their inputs had any real impact. If the idea has merit and can be implemented utilizing the resources that are available, then great amounts of trust, pride, and ownership will be reaped if the idea is implemented. Trust and ownership are critical components necessary to move the organization further down the leadership progression (Styles 3 and 4).

Of course, trust can also evaporate quickly if the request for help is only a façade. Old style managers will sometimes try to deceive others into thinking they are trying to create a new culture of collaboration. They will ask employees for their ideas with no real intention of using any of these inputs. Or they will pull together groups of employees to make suggestions on ways to improve a process and then the participants realize that there was never any intention of using their inputs. These fake teams may even discover that while they have been working on an improvement idea, the manager has already decided to do something entirely different. Unfortunately, this has happened several times in my own career.

In one example, I was part of a group that had been brought together to discuss and change a key policy the company executives wanted updated. This policy had far-reaching ramifications throughout the enterprise. We were asked to go off-site for 5 days to discuss alternatives, and the CEO of the company wanted to hear our recommendations on the final day. On the third day, our meeting was interrupted by a rather tall, mysterious looking man who introduced himself as one of the Corporate Vice Presidents. He wanted to know what we were planning to present to his boss. We walked him through our recommendations and he intently listened. After we shared our thoughts, he got up from his chair, walked over to where we had all of our flipchart papers and began pulling the charts off of the wall and dropped them down to the floor. He explained that what we were going to recommend was totally unacceptable and that he would help us come up with the right solution. He then went over to one of the flip chart stands and began crafting several pages of recommendations. As he left the room, he told us that it would be best for our future careers if we presented his plan exactly as it was written on the flip chart pages. Of course, the group of participants was stunned and speechless. We realized that this meeting was nothing more than a sham and several participants said that they would never volunteer to be a part of any future idea generation groups.

Friday came and we reluctantly presented to the CEO everything the tall man had wanted us to show. The leader of our company said, "I am really disappointed. What you just presented is similar to the tired, outdated drivel my staff tells me. I was hoping this team would come up with some new, creative ideas." Our group leader (the bravery of this person really stuck with me throughout my career) told our CEO that we did have some other ideas. He then unrolled all of the flip chart papers that contained what we had discussed during the first part of the week and shared these ideas with the attendees. After this part of the presentation, our CEO exclaimed, "Now that is what I was hoping for! I want to implement these ideas right away." The tall man was sitting in the audience and I noticed that his face turned a bright red as his anger swelled. Fortunately, this person left the company soon after this meeting took place.

Other examples I have witnessed of managers using fake teams do not have positive endings. In one, a group I was working with was asked to provide ideas on a new way to lay out their workspace. This was a 3-day, off-site meeting. Late on the second day, the participants decided to make a surprise visit to the office in order to get some measurements. While there, they discovered that the manager had already begun installing a design he had arrived at on his own and had no intention of utilizing any of the recommendations. The formation of this group (and the use of our time) was all a scam to try and make the manager look like he cared about the participants' input. It was all a façade. After this realization, several of the employees swore that they would never volunteer to be part of another improvement project.

If a Style 1 leader is sincere about moving the organization to the Fact Gathering Leader (Style 2) and truly wants input from employees on ways to improve, then they need to be ready, willing, and able to implement several of the ideas that are produced. Even if an idea does not move the ball forward much, the mere fact that the worker can see evidence that their input was respected will go a long way toward building trust between the leaders and the workers. This will begin to develop critical thinking skills within the workforce and there will be a sense of pride that begins to emerge.

For example, in one organization, a group of workers were asked for their thoughts on ways their process could improve. Several of these ideas were implemented and this led to more ideas being expressed. I facilitated several of these meetings and when I left, this particular group of employees was fully engaged in making improvements throughout their area of the business. A few months later, I had the opportunity to return to see how things were going. This group of workers met me at the front door and excitedly began to share a rather long list of improvements that had been made based on their inputs. The pride was beaming in each of their faces as they escorted me to several locations to showcase their efforts. They made it clear that they would make sure that their processes ran as smoothly as possible. This is the power of getting the workers engaged and an easy way to accomplish this is to ask for (and implement some of) their ideas. The more input that is utilized, the greater the ownership for what happens in the organization.

Of course, not all ideas can be implemented (or are even worthy of consideration). A skilled Style 2 – Fact Gathering Leader knows that it is important to treat these less than desirable ideas in the correct manner. If mishandled, the employees will naturally assume that the effort was faked. This will result in a further erosion of trust. What can be done to minimize the chance of this happening? First, treat all ideas with tremendous respect. The person who offered this input was most likely sincere and somewhat brave to provide their idea. The leader will need to treat this input with great care. Do not cross the idea off of a list or throw the card that the idea is written on into the trash. This shows great disrespect. Instead, explain to the employee why it is not the appropriate time to implement their idea, thank them for the input, and then ask them to keep thinking of new ways to move the ball forward. Also explain that if things change, their idea may still be valid and may be considered at a later date. I have seen this happen several times; an idea that seemed laughable turns into a valid improvement project a year or two later once a few other improvements are made.

The leader does need to make it clear though that the final decision will rest on their shoulders. This removes any concern about the liability associated with an improvement project that goes badly. Also, this is a good point in the organization's progression toward collaboration to begin providing training to all of the employees. The first round of ideas will probably be simple, common sense inputs that are fairly easy to implement. However, after these easy improvements are made, the next round of projects may require more in-depth critical thinking skills. I am a firm believer that every employee would benefit from going through training on the various improvement tools and methodologies (be sure to sign up a trainer who uses hands-on training techniques). This begins to develop a common language among all of the workers, and the fear of improvement and change begins to melt. This will help the organization move toward Style 3 – The Team Forming Leader.

MISSION, VISION, STRATEGY, AND VALUES

There seems to be much confusion as to the difference between Mission, Vision, Strategy, and Values. The definitions I use when working with an organization might be slightly different than the industry-expected norms. However, feedback has been positive and organizations have shared that the definitions listed below helped them achieve clarity on their journey toward excellence. Remember, the goal here is to utilize these tools to actually help plan the future path that the organization will take in order to make things better. This is not meant to be an exercise that wastes people's time and all of the information is put into a binder that sits on a shelf.

What exactly is meant by Mission, Vision, Strategy, and Values?

> *Mission – Why do we exist as an organization? What is our purpose? Why do the people we serve (customers, patients, constituents, etc.) value what we do?*

Vision – A description of the future that will inspire and excite everyone within the organization to be a part of something greater than the current normal. This provides a path forward that will help keep the organization relevant to the people we serve and guide us toward fulfilling our Mission.

Strategy – What actions do we need to complete in order to make the vision a reality? How do we prioritize the use of our resources (people, time, financial) to move toward this new future reality?

Values – How would we describe the organization's culture, that which is considered critically important to the successful implementation of the strategy in the most efficient and effective way? What evidence is there that these values are actually being demonstrated throughout the organization?

As you can see from the descriptions, each of these four characteristics builds on the one before. In other words, the vision describes a future that supports the mission, the strategy consists of the steps to implement the vision, and the values describe how the organization will work together to achieve the strategy. If one of these four traits is missing, the entire chain falls apart. For example, it is difficult to put a strategy together if the organization has no idea where it is going or why it even exists. On the other hand, a group can have a powerful mission but fail miserably if it has no vision of where it is going or a plan of how to get there.

These four direction-setting organizational characteristics match up with the Leadership Progression Model (Figure 6.1).

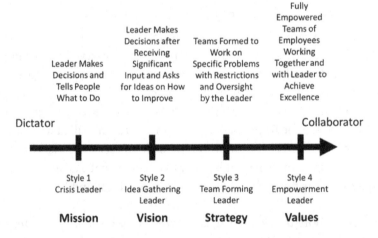

FIGURE 6.1
Direction Setting with Leadership Progression Model.

STYLE 1 – CRISIS LEADER AND MISSION

Since the Style 1 – Crisis Leader will be making most, if not all, of the decisions, the only thing that is important for the rest of the organization to understand is the mission: why do we exist? This will help clarify to the employees why there is a crisis and help reinforce the need to make the changes that are being mandated by the leader. Since the mission of the organization does not usually change from year to year, having the mission defined, communicated, and well understood by the employees before a crisis hits will make the difficult situation easier to navigate for the Crisis Leader. Without a well-understood mission, the Crisis Leader may come across as making random, chaotic decisions that will frustrate the employees at all levels in the organization.

STYLE 2 – IDEA GATHERING LEADER AND VISION

As was seen in the story portion of this chapter, without a vision, the Style 2 – Idea Gathering Leader (Jim) will run into problems when seeking inputs from the rest of the organization. If the vision is to introduce a new, completely redesigned version of a current product, for example, then ideas on how to improve the current design will not have nearly the impact that might be expected. This is especially true for ideas that would take longer to implement than the life of the current offering. Frustration can result, especially for the employees who might have put a great deal of thought and effort into coming up with these ideas. It is critically important that the Idea Gathering Leader, along with their leadership team, craft a vision of the future, share this vision with all of the employees, and get buy-in and commitment from the employees to support this new direction. The way to get this buy-in is to allow the employees (along with customers and suppliers) to contribute to the creation of this vision. This can be a powerful process since it will teach the entire organization how to think about the future in a positive way.

STYLE 3 – TEAM FORMING LEADER AND STRATEGY

When it is time to begin setting up teams of employees, the Style 3 – Team Forming Leader will want a strategy crafted and well thought out.

The strategy will need to define the steps required to turn the vision into something real. This will help to prioritize what the initial employee teams will need to focus on first. For example, if one of the steps in the strategy is to fix unsafe work conditions in a specific part of the process, then it would make sense to form an employee team to specifically address these concerns. Too many times, I have seen organizations begin forming employee teams with no real plan that defines the priorities. This can lead to great frustration, especially when a team has success and then realizes that their work will have little to no impact because they were focused on something that was not part of the overall strategy.

STYLE 4 – EMPOWERMENT LEADER AND VALUES

For those organizations and their leaders who are able to make it to Style 4 – Empowerment Leader, having a common understanding of the key, critical values required to be successful will be paramount to achieving excellence. Once these values have been defined, it will still take significant amounts of time and effort to change the culture of the organization. However, defining these values will begin to build a roadmap that can help lay out the way employees at all levels will interact with each other. One note on values: it is easy to define what the values of the organization should be. However, it is usually much more difficult to consistently demonstrate and embrace these values. When an organization explains to me what their key values are, I like to ask them to share concrete, specific examples. If this is difficult, then the values are still a wish list and have not become part of the culture. Also, if the leaders are not willing to change their own behaviors in order to make a specific value a reality, then they run the risk of creating a façade that the rest of the organization will soon be able to see through.

We will go into more depth regarding Missions and Visions now and go deeper into Strategy and Values in a later chapter.

MISSION AND VISION

Mission – Why do we exist as an organization? What is our purpose? Why do the people we serve (customers, patients, constituents, etc.) value what we do?

Most people are aware of something called a "mission statement." My experience is that when crafting a mission statement, 10% of the time (or less) is spent on the content and 90%+ is spent on wordsmithing the statement so it sounds good on a business card. These percentages need to flip so that the majority of the time is spent on defining the soul of the organization. Once a mission statement is written, it should not need to change much unless the organization decides to go in a radically new direction. There may be a need to tweak the language from time to time. If your organization's mission is "to provide the best rotary phones ever made" then it is way past time to update the purpose (a business with this mission statement is most likely already bankrupt).

There should not be a need to change the organization's mission when a new leader comes on board unless this person was hired to take the group in an entirely new direction. If this is the case, then the employees will need to recognize the fact that they are no longer working for the same organization even though the name of the company may stay the same. Keeping the mission statement from boss to boss assumes, of course, that the original mission was well crafted and is reflective of the true purpose. If this is not the case, then a new leader may need to scrap the old statement entirely and, with the help of the leadership team, come up with a mission statement that is more accurate and reflective of what the organization is meant to be about.

What can cause mission statements to be ineffective drivel? They can be too broad ("We strive to be the best at everything") or too narrow ("Paperclips are our passion"). Maybe the statement isn't particularly inspirational ("Our focus is to survive by not making too many mistakes") or is just total nonsense ("Our success depends on being successful"). The goal of a good mission statement is to help the employees, suppliers, customers, shareholders, executives, and even competitors answer the all-important question, "Why does this organization exist?" This then becomes "True North" on the compass to help guide the entire organization forward. Everyone will then better understand why certain decisions get made. This will help reduce the chance of conflicts and surprises.

What is an example of a sound mission statement? Think about the following: "The American Red Cross prevents and alleviates human suffering in the face of emergencies by mobilizing the power of volunteers and the generosity of donors." Does this statement explain why the American Red Cross exists? Is it inspirational? Does it explain the value the organization brings to those it serves? The statement passes all of these requirements and will serve as a great guide for this massive non-profit entity. For example, if an employee proposed an idea such as, "Let's get into the grocery business and launch a chain of stores," the leaders of the American Red Cross will be able to easily explain that this idea does not fit with their fundamental identity outlined in their mission statement.

Vision – A description of the future that will inspire and excite everyone within the organization to be a part of something greater than the current normal. This provides a path forward that will help keep the organization relevant to the people we serve and guide us toward fulfilling our Mission.

Crafting an effective vision of the future can be a daunting task. My experience is that most organizations do not bother with this step or do a poor job. However, I think this is one of the most critical steps required to achieve excellence. Asking the organization to think about the future does two important things. First, it will help to set the stage that change is important in order to stay relevant. Second, it will focus everyone on a new, hopefully better, future that will diminish the petty issues and concerns of the past. Discussing an inspirational vision of the future will begin to tap into the wonderment of what is possible.

The steps required to create a vision are:

1) The leadership team will need to make sure that an effective mission statement has been created and is well understood by the entire organization.
2) Inputs are then gathered from the employees, customers, suppliers, supervisors, and executives as to what needs to be in place 2 to 3 years from now that will help the organization achieve its mission.
3) The leadership team will then process these inputs by putting them into various categories and themes. This will help clarify areas of the organization that could benefit the most by making changes to support this future vision.
4) The leadership team will then put together a description of an inspirational future that can rally the employees around this new vision. This can be a statement or a set of bullet points and will need to be as specific and descriptive as possible.
5) This new vision will then need to be communicated throughout the organization (with feedback and possibly some revisions) in order to get buy-in and ownership.
6) A set of specific actions will then be developed in order to begin the process of turning this vision into a reality (Strategy).

Some guidelines when creating a vision:

- Keep the customer in the middle of all vision discussions. "What would the people we serve like to see us accomplish over the next 2 to 3 years?"
- Avoid using results type statements such as, "We want to double our profits in the next 3 years." This is not a vision. The vision consists of specific things that would need to be in place in order to better serve the customer. A vision well-crafted and implemented will lead to better results.
- Don't discount any ideas. Outlandish thoughts might lead to breakthrough thinking that could result in a new vision that has never been considered before.

Finally, one way to turn an idea into a vision is to ask, several times, the question, "And then what?" in order to see if this idea will eventually help with the overall mission. For example, a local government organization, with a mission of revitalizing their downtown, might have a vision of putting a bandstand in the middle of their town square. If we assume that this vision becomes a reality, what happens next (we build the bandstand, *and then what?*)? It would be easy to then describe a cool summer evening where many families gather on blankets with baskets of food and drink ready to listen to a variety of music being played by a band the town hired to entertain on this new bandstand.... *And then what?* Several of these families decide to spend time shopping at local establishments that are near the park, buying ice cream, browsing through racks of clothes, and contemplating buying pieces of art and furniture while continuing to listen to the music drifting in from the bandstand.... *And then what?* After several of these evening concerts, the local businesses begin to turn a profit, which then invites more entrepreneurs to move their businesses into empty stores. This leads to a new revitalization of the town which would begin to fulfill the town's mission.

In the book of Proverbs, written over 2,500 years ago, there is a verse that goes: "Where there is no vision, the people perish." The same can be said about any organization. Taking the time to discuss what can be possible, even if things do not unfold exactly as described, creates a sense of excitement that will help energize any organization toward achieving excellence.

7

Style Three Leadership – Team Forming Leader

Teamwork is so much more than putting a group of people in a room and saying, "be a team"

THE STORY OF JIM BROWN

Mary Robinson had worked as a production employee for the JED Company for over 10 years. For the first time, she was beginning to feel a glimmer of hope and optimism. Two months had passed since Susan Jones, the director of operations, visited Mary's workstation to ask her for input on how to improve. True to Susan's word, she visited almost every day with updates on progress that was being made to implement several of Mary's ideas. Some of these suggestions did not produce the results she expected, but most of them had a positive impact. In the past, Mary's process would routinely shut down other areas of the business due to quality and output issues. It had been 14 days since there was an outage and Mary could not be more thrilled to have finally moved the spotlight of ineptitude away from her part of the process. Jim Brown, the new V.P. of this division, even came down from his corner office to thank Mary for her ideas and congratulate her on the improvements. Not everything was rosy by any means. There were still problems that needed to be dealt with, but the extra capacity realized by making the improvements gave her process a chance to catch up before too much damage was done.

A few weeks ago, during one of Susan's visits, she had asked Mary if she would be interested in attending a training class that covered several process improvement tools and methodologies. She reluctantly agreed. On the day of the training, Mary felt overwhelmed when she entered the classroom and saw several of the company leaders in attendance. "What have I gotten myself into?" she thought at the time. Then she noticed that Jim Brown and Susan Jones were also there. "Wait a minute," thought Mary. "Are they here as participants?!? Wow! They are taking time away from their jobs to be a part of this training as well. This must be a bigger deal than I thought." In the introduction ice breaker, Jim Brown had mentioned that one of his hobbies was fly fishing and that he took great joy in tying his own flies. Mary and her husband also enjoyed fly fishing on the river that passed by her mother's house. At lunch on the first day of the class, Mary sat by Jim and swapped several fantastic fish stories that grew bigger with each tale. The laughter from their end of the table was contagious and the entire class began to listen and share their own fish stories. "I can't believe what I am hearing," Mary thought at the time. "Jim, Susan, and the other executives are real people with similar interests. I never in my wildest dreams would have thought that we would have so much in common."

The class was actually fun and engaging and covered several topics. Mary especially enjoyed the many hands-on activities that brought home all of the key learning points. These lessons had a real impact. She began to realize that maybe there was a better way to get things done and that when something went wrong, it was better to blame the process instead of jumping to the conclusion that it was a worker's or leader's fault. "These are tools that my husband and I could actually use to organize and improve what we do on our farm back home," Mary shared with the group at the end of the class. "I really appreciate being a part of this training and will be sure to share with the other workers that they need to attend with an open mind when it is their turn."

Two weeks later, Susan and Jim both stopped by Mary's workstation. Jim gave her a gift, a fly fishing fly that Jim had personally tied. "Wait a minute," Mary said after admiring the craftsmanship. "Are there any strings attached to this gift? Are you about to ask me for more ideas on how to improve?"

"Well, in a way, yes," said Jim. "I mean, no, there are no strings attached to the gift. I wanted you to have this as a way to say thanks for being one of the first workers to get out of their comfort zone and begin the process of making improvement happen. However, Susan and I would like to ask you to consider taking the next step on our improvement journey."

"We have decided to form our first employee improvement team and we would like you to be one of the members," said Susan. "This new team will be asked to focus on a significant problem that is beginning to have a negative impact on our business. Our customer call center is struggling to keep up with the numerous calls they are receiving. The average time our customers are on hold waiting for someone to answer is now over 28 minutes."

"Remember that this is the average time, so some of our customers are waiting for almost an hour," added Jim. "In the past, we had similar call volumes and the same number of customer representatives was able to keep up. Something has changed and we have gotten significantly worse in this key metric. We want this new team to use some of the tools we learned in the training to help us identify wasteful parts of the process and come up with ideas on ways to be more efficient without impacting the service our customers receive."

"Wait a minute," said Mary with disbelief in her voice. "I don't know anything about the customer call center. I am not sure that I have ever even set foot in that part of the business. What could I possibly contribute?"

"We need someone on the team who has never worked in that part of the process," said Susan. "Someone who can bring a fresh perspective and challenge the old ways of doing things. You have such good ideas and we thought that you would be the right person to try out the new tools and methodologies."

"I don't know," said Mary. "I had 10 years to think about my part of the process and determine ways to make it better. That won't be the case with the customer call center. I will give it a try, but don't expect anything too great from my contributions."

"Fantastic!" said Jim. "Thank you and don't worry. Every team needs at least one or two people who can bring a new perspective to an old process. I bet there will be questions you ask that others in this group will also want to know the answers to but are too afraid to ask."

Mary later found out that the first team meeting was going to be held off-site at one of the nicer hotels in their local city. "My, my, my!" thought Mary as she looked at the vaulted ceilings and stained glass windows of the hotel lobby when she arrived. "This place is amazing." Fear began to creep in as Mary became overwhelmed by it all. "What have I done? Why did I agree to this?" Several times on her way to the meeting room, Mary almost turned around to run back to her car and drive home. "I can't let Jim and Susan down," she kept repeating in her mind, and this gave her the courage to enter the meeting.

"Ah, here she is," said a man who was standing in the middle of the conference room. "You must be Mary. There is an empty seat over here.

Thank you so much for your willingness to be a part of this team. My name is Kyle and I will be providing facilitation for this meeting."

"Facilitation?" asked Mary. "I am sorry to be ignorant of how all of this works."

"Don't worry Mary," said one of the other participants. "I was wondering what that meant as well. Thank you for asking."

"I am here to help you all through the process of solving the problem you have been asked to work on," said Kyle. "A facilitator is a neutral person who does not get into the content of the meeting but instead focuses on the process. So, anything I can do to help you all be successful is why I am here."

There were a total of 12 people in the room and Mary was fairly certain that she was the only one, other than Kyle, who did not work in the Customer Service department. Mary stayed mostly quiet throughout the first half of the meeting.

The group began working on creating a Process Map of the current way they answer the calls coming in from their customers. Mary remembered from the training that Process Mapping was a tool that created a picture of the process so each participant would have a common understanding of what was really going on. Each step was written on an index card and taped to paper that had been attached to the wall. The steps they had identified so far were pretty basic: the phone rings; the customer rep answers and greets the customer; the customer shares their question or concern; the customer rep records the data into the computer and looks up the information; the customer rep shares information with the customer; if customer is satisfied then the rep thanks them for the call and hangs up; if customer is not satisfied then the rep passes the call on to a supervisor.

"I have a question," said Mary. Since this was one of the first times Mary had spoken, the rest of the participants quieted down and gave Mary the floor. "Earlier, several of you mentioned that you work on e-mail requests for information from customers between calls. If you are in the middle of researching the answer to an e-mail question and the phone rings, how does that impact things?"

"It absolutely blows this process up!" blurted out one of the call-takers. "The e-mail system is completely different than the call-taking system so we have to stop what we were doing, close all of the e-mail screens, and then launch the call-taking program. Our computers are so old that if you don't make this switch in exactly the right way, the entire computer shuts down and has to be restarted."

"Yeah, I hate to admit this," said another participant, "and I hope this stays in this room or my career might be over, but I actually turn my phone off when I get asked to work on e-mails."

"How many of you all do the same thing?" asked Kyle. All of the customer reps' hands went up.

"Wow," said Mary. "No wonder customers are on hold for so long. I think that this needs to be added to our map." The other participants gasped and shook their heads with a look of horror on their faces. "Don't worry. I have spoken to our V.P. Jim Brown several times and he celebrates breakthroughs like this. He wants us to identify the ugly parts of the process... and this is really ugly. We can only improve after we admit that there are problems." Mary walked up to the wall where the Process Map hung and started adding cards (Figure 7.1).

The group was not completely sold that this was smart, but Mary kept reassuring them that Jim Brown would celebrate these revelations. One by one, the customer representatives began to share the ugly steps of their part of the process and the map continued to grow with all of the workarounds that were required to get the job done. By the time they had finished, the process map had over 90 steps and covered most of the conference room wall. The participants were shocked by how ugly their process looked and began to realize that things were far worse than any one of them had originally thought. This epiphany opened the door to the possibilities of changing the process to try and improve the way things were done.

"I was thinking we would come out of this meeting with a recommendation to hire more people," said one of the participants, "but it is now clear to me that we have a ton of waste and inefficiencies in our process. We definitely need to clean this up."

When they got to the part of the meeting agenda that focused on discussing solutions, Mary once again spoke up. "Wouldn't it make sense

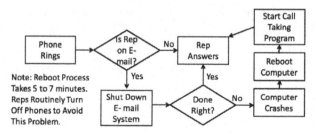

FIGURE 7.1
Process Map of Call-Taking Process.

to upgrade everyone's computers so you can have both systems running at the same time?"

"We don't have the budget for that massive of an upgrade this year," replied one of the customer service leaders. "Maybe we could ask for these funds in next year's budget."

"Okay, it does not sound like we can wait that long before making some substantial improvements," said Mary. "What would happen if you dedicate… say 25% of the customer reps to doing the e-mail requests and the other 75% focus on answering the phones? Wouldn't that eliminate most of the problem with switching between the two?"

"That would work if we had a consistent inflow of requests, but it fluctuates too much," replied one of the participants.

"Maybe you could 'flex' people. We learned in our training class that it helps to even out the flow of a process by having several workers cross-trained to be able to do multiple jobs and then fill in where needed to keep the process moving," suggested Mary.

"Hmmm… that might work," said the leader of the group. "We have enough in our budget to upgrade the computer systems of a handful of workers. We could have part of our people dedicated to e-mail requests, part dedicated to phone call taking, and then a few who work on e-mails and then switch to taking calls if needed. That will save a ton of wasted time."

The rest of the group agreed and ultimately reached consensus with several of their improvement ideas including the one Mary suggested. They pitched their ideas to Jim Brown and the director of their department. True to Mary's word, Jim was thrilled when he saw all of the ugly steps in the process and congratulated the team. He agreed with the team's recommendations and gave them a green light to try out their ideas. It did not take long to buy and set up new computers and program the phone system to create two dedicated teams and a flex group. The impact of this improvement, as well as several others that were made, was immediately felt by their customers and the average "on hold" time began to drop from 28 minutes to a little over 2 minutes. After several weeks of consistently demonstrating this performance level, the entire department had a lunch to celebrate. They invited Mary and made her an honorary customer service rep. She and the others who participated in the off-site meeting could not wait to get back together to offer more ideas of how to improve the call-taking process even further in order to achieve real excellence.

THE STORY OF FRANK SMITH

On the other side of the state, Frank was having another bad day. First, his boss had told him to start asking the wretched workers for their ideas and now he was told to pull a group of employees together to begin improving their process. His boss shared with him the "amazing" improvements made over at Jim Brown's part of the business in their customer service center. "Can you believe they were able to reduce the average customer on-hold time by over 90%?" his boss had said. "That is pretty impressive. I know that your metrics have also been improving, especially the quality numbers going over 98%. Maybe you can share how you were able to improve your quality and they can share how they were able to improve their customer service performance."

"Humph," thought Frank. "I will show them how much better we can be in our own customer service center." He called together a couple of his top lieutenants and directed them to pull together a group of employees. When this new team held their first meeting, Frank decided to say a few words in order to inspire them to achieve excellence.

"As you know, you have been called together to try and figure out how to reduce the amount of time our customers are on hold when they call into our customer care center," Frank began at their first meeting. "Currently, the average amount of time our customers wait before someone answers their call is over 24 minutes. This is totally unacceptable. Clearly, we have a bunch of lazy call-takers who do not care about this business or their jobs. I fully expect that the average on-hold time to be less than a minute by this time next week or heads will roll beginning with the people in this room. Do I make myself perfectly clear?"

With a great deal of hesitancy, one of the participants raised her hand to ask a question. "Do we have a budget to fund process changes?"

"No," replied Frank bluntly. "We don't need to make too many changes to this process. This customer care center has been around for several decades and it was doing just fine in the past. My expectation is that you will figure out a way to light a fire under the workers' behinds in order to make them more productive. That does not cost any money. I will be making one investment that you will see in the next day or two. A large electronic sign will go up that shows the actual on-hold data in real time. That will help you determine if you are being successful with your improvements. Are there any other questions?"

The group stared down at the table in front of them and did not speak. Frank took that as a sign that he was no longer needed and he left the room. The leader of the group said, "So, basically, what I heard from our boss is that we have no money, can't really change anything, and this all has to be done by next week or we are all fired. Any suggestions on what we can do to get out of this mess?"

"I really need this job!" shouted one of the participants a bit too loudly. "We have got to do something dramatic and do it quick."

With no real agenda or facilitator to help, this group of employees sat mostly in silence until the allotted time was up and they returned to their work desks. The next day, a crew came in and installed the big electronic board Frank had told them about. This sign reminded the workers of a scoreboard one might see at a basketball game. The digital numbers showed the current wait time of their customers and when this number went above 60 seconds, lights started flashing and a buzzer went off to let everyone know they were over the goal.

Later that day, the group that had met previously got together to discuss next steps. "First, we have got to figure out how to turn off that stupid buzzer," said the leader.

"We can stuff some rags into the speakers and that will stop most of the noise," offered one of the participants. "Also, I think I might have an idea on how we can reduce our wait times. When we answer the phone, if the problem the customer is having will take more than a minute to address, let's pretend that we have a bad connection and hang up on them. That will greatly reduce the amount of time our operators are on the phone and will allow them to take more calls."

The rest of the group was pretty disgusted with this suggestion but they finally had to admit that they had no other answers. The next day, the leader informed the rest of the customer call center reps about their idea and that Frank had told them everyone would be fired if they did not get to the 1-minute goal. The workers reluctantly agreed to give this idea a try. The average time did drop but not enough to meet Frank's objective. The lights on the scoreboard kept flashing and the buzzer, although now muffled, kept buzzing.

"Okay. Drastic times call for drastic measures," said one of the participants at the next group meeting. "We brought down the wait times but not enough to satisfy Frank. I propose that when we see the hold time metric on Frank's scoreboard go above 30 seconds, we begin the process of picking up the phone and putting it back down in order to hang up on the customer. This is the only way we are going to keep our jobs."

"Won't this thoroughly tick off our customers?" asked one of the participants with horror in her voice.

"They will just think that they have a bad connection or that their cell phone dropped the call. We are running out of time. Frank said we had to be below 1 minute by tomorrow or we will all be fired. Can anyone think of another idea?" The group slowly shook their heads.

A few days later, Frank was beaming with pride when he picked up the phone to call his boss. "We now have 34-second wait times! Tell Jim Brown that he can stuff his division's 2-minute performance. Maybe they are not doing that great after all!" After his boss congratulated him, Frank hung up the phone and thought, "Achieving excellence feels so good! Hmmm... Now that the hold times are well below the original target, maybe it is time to get rid of some of the operators. The customers can wait a bit longer. Achieving excellence and saving money! Things are finally looking up."

PRACTICAL APPLICATIONS

In the story portion of this chapter, Jim and Susan introduce the Style 3 – Team Forming Leader. In my experience, this is the step in the leadership progression that begins to separate those executives who truly want their organization to achieve excellence and those who are trying to do the minimum amount of work in order to perpetuate the façade. This step requires a great deal of focus, determination, and support by every leader in the organization. There is a misperception that all that is required in forming a team is to throw a group of people into a room, give them a task, and they will naturally start acting like a team. This is rarely the case. In order to achieve real teamwork, several key ingredients are required and if these are not present, the team will eventually fail. If this happens, the skeptics will claim that the improvement efforts were not successful and this will become an excuse to move the organization back to "old style" management... the comfort zone for many in the organization.

What are the key ingredients needed to promote successful teams?

1) *A common understanding of the organization's Mission, Vision, and Strategy* – Each team that is formed will have a far greater chance to get the time, resources, and support it needs if it is clear why the success of this team is critical to achieving the strategy that supports

arriving at the vision. Too many times, I have seen teams get thrown together and then they are given a task that has little or no impact on the future success of the organization. This is usually done in order for the manager to check off a box that meets a personal objective with no intention of allowing the team to have any real impact. I remember, several years ago, encountering a team that was put together in order to decide what type of plants would work best in the employee cafeteria and another team that was assigned the task of coordinating employee birthday celebrations. I doubt that these teams' actions would help the organization achieve their strategy but it did allow management to say that they were utilizing teams.

Another reason why it is critically important for the team to understand where they fit into the overall strategy: participants want to know if the time serving on the team is valued or wasted. I have had the opportunity to work with several dozens of teams throughout my career and one of the main causes of people exhibiting disruptive behaviors in a team meeting is the lack of a valid answer to the question, "Why am I here?" Team participants are usually under significant pressure to get their day jobs done and if there is a belief that the team they have been asked to serve on is not all that important, then they will become disruptive. These disruptions take on many forms such as showing up late (if at all), taking phone calls in the middle of the meeting, trying to go off on a tangent in order to get real work done, and not working on any of the assigned tasks since these are viewed as low priorities. These disruptions, especially without a facilitator, will usually result in the team becoming frustrated and eventually falling apart.

2) *The use of a well-trained, neutral facilitator* – In the early 1990s, General Electric launched a team initiative that was titled "Work Out." This was a companywide initiative that was put into place in order to start getting teams of employees together to "work out" problems. It was a requirement in many parts of the company that each of these teams have a trained, neutral facilitator. In most cases, even the most difficult teams were able to achieve positive results due to the presence of a facilitator.

What exactly is the role of a facilitator? As was mentioned in the story portion of this chapter, a facilitator is there to help the team be successful. They do not get into the content but instead focus on the meeting process. This means that before the meeting, the facilitator will make sure there is an agenda, that there is a clear definition of what success looks like, and that the scope of the problem is well defined and the appropriate people have been invited. During the meeting, they will follow a plan that will help improve the odds that the participants will come together as a team (ice breakers and team building exercises), provide tools to help the team analyze the data and reach conclusions, and assist with helping the team reach consensus on a way forward. Consensus is achieved when all of the team members reach an agreement that might not have been their first choice, but is acceptable to them in order to move onward with a recommendation.

In order to help the teams achieve positive outcomes, it is critically important that the facilitator be neutral. If there is a perception that the facilitator is trying to sway the group toward a specific outcome, then the team will think that the meeting is fake and that management placed a spy in the room in order to make sure the team reaches the conclusion that the managers want. So, the best facilitator is one who is outside of the department, division, or even outside of the entire organization. Keep in mind that only teams who have been brought together to make significant decisions need a facilitator. Also, as the team gains experience working together and making decisions, the need for a facilitator will diminish. The use of truly neutral facilitators is the strongest indicator that the organization has a Style 3 leader who is willing to make the necessary investments to move the organization toward collaboration.

3) *All team members have been trained on the tools and methodologies of making improvement happen* – Again, it amazes me how many times an organization will throw a group of employees together, with little to no training, and expect them to come together as a team and solve a difficult problem. If the managers are unwilling to make the investment of time and resources to help their employees gain the skills needed to work together to make improvement happen, then their goal of achieving excellence will eventually fail.

Training also will provide the teams the tools and methodologies they will need to work on complex problems. A common saying is: "If the problems were easy to fix, they would have been dealt with long ago." There are many tools available to help a team better understand their process (Process Maps, Spaghetti Diagrams), display data in order to better understand what is happening (Histograms, Run

Charts, Scatter Diagrams), and analyze the data in order to make a recommendation for a solution (Root Cause Analysis, Statistical Process Control (SPC)). There are also several methodologies that will provide a roadmap for the teams to better understand the steps needed in order to have the best chance of success. The most common methodology is known as Plan, Do, Check, Act – PDCA (some use Plan, Do, Study, Act – PDSA). This is a simple, four-step approach that assures that the teams follow a prescribed formula when making changes. Most organizations understand the importance of putting a plan together before changing something. However, with everyone's busy schedules, there is a temptation to implement the plan and then provide no follow-up to see if the desired outcome has been achieved. By not following the PDCA cycle, the improvement efforts have a greater chance of failure, which will eventually destroy the teams. Proper training and dedication to using the appropriate tools and methodologies will lessen the chance that this will happen.

4) *Avoid using the wrong tools and techniques when making decisions* – There are many ways that a team can implode and achieve poor or even negative results. Training will help the teams better understand the pitfalls to avoid and provide assistance when problems do occur. Also, the teams can avoid utilizing techniques that will assure their destruction if they are aware of these hazards. For example, there is one decision technique that will guarantee that the team will splinter, fall apart, and then completely and utterly fail. This decision technique is voting. When a vote occurs, the team now consists of "winners" and "losers." No one wants to be a loser. The losers of the vote will do everything in their power to make sure that the decision does not work and then will tell the majority who won the vote that they were wrong and should have voted their way. This causes great friction within the team, leading to eventual failure. If the leaders of the organization truly want their teams to be successful, then they would provide training and a neutral facilitator to make sure that the participants avoid these types of mistakes.

5) *The teams have all of the necessary data and resources to make the best possible decisions* – "Knowledge is power" is a well-known saying. Some managers are reluctant to give up their data to a team since this is a step toward giving up their power. This is why the Style 3 leadership step in the Progression Model is a real test of the organization's desire to achieve collaboration that is necessary

in order to realize its vision of excellence. I have been told several times in my career that the data the team is seeking is proprietary or that the company cannot afford the possibility that the data is leaked to a competitor or to the customers. In many of these cases, the data turned out to be common knowledge in the industry and it became clear that the manager did not want to diminish their power by allowing others to have access to this knowledge.

Another way managers can limit the ability of the employee teams to get much done is to starve them of the necessary resources to make anything happen. I have encountered many examples of teams that come up with ideas that will actually save the company significant money with little investment, yet the managers can't seem to find the funds or free up the resources needed to make the necessary changes. If this is the case, it would have been better to not begin the teams in the first place. Not being able to implement their ideas will cause frustration and will eventually lead the team members to think that the use of teams is all a façade.

There are several key resources that would benefit the team if they were a part of the improvement process. One resource that every team needs is a good accounting person who is connected to the financial department of the organization. Calculating savings associated with making improvements can be difficult and having someone with a financial background can lend credibility to these calculations. Each team also needs a sponsor, someone who is in the leadership ranks who can make sure that the team is directly plugged into the strategy and vision of the organization. The sponsor can help make sure that the team members have sufficient time to meet, that a facilitator is provided, and that the scope of what the team is working on is well understood. The sponsor can also make sure that any roadblocks are dealt with and that resources and funding are provided to implement the team's recommendations. In many cases, the Style 3 – Team Forming Leader will be the sponsor themselves, especially early on in the improvement process.

6) *The final ingredient for successful teams: Don't do stupid stuff* – This final ingredient is the most important so I will repeat it: *Don't Do Stupid Stuff!* One sure way to stop all team activity and destroy any hope of achieving excellence is to fire employees due to an improvement project. Unfortunately, this happens all too often. Frank Smith in the story went down this path. Since most of the examples in the

story portions of this book are based on actual examples, it would be correct to conclude that the illustration of call-takers hanging up phones in order to cut the hold times of their customers is possible. The result of this fake improvement was that almost half of the call-takers were let go from the organization. You can only imagine the chaotic mess that was created when management discovered that the improvements were faked and customer complaints skyrocketed.

Why is firing employees due to improvements (or even the perception that the firings were due to improvements) so destructive? If a team recommends a change that results in a peer, friend, or even themselves being let go from the organization, no one will ever volunteer to be on another improvement team. This will hamper team efforts for years, maybe even decades and the amount of trust between employees and management will drop to zero.

The organization's leaders will need to make a sincere commitment to not fire anyone due to an improvement being implemented. Employees can still be let go due to a downturn in the economy (this must be thoroughly explained to the workforce or trust will still evaporate) or for cause. If an improvement does reduce or eliminate the need for workers in that part of the process, then the leaders will need to work diligently to find them a new home and let attrition slowly reduce the workforce to appropriate levels. If there aren't any open positions currently available, then temporary jobs may need to be created, possibly a job doing improvements on a full-time basis.

Also, leaders will need to look at the cause and effect of all of the team's recommendations for improvement. In one plant, a team's improvement plan almost triggered a riot. At the time, we thought that this team was working on something that should have been a positive with everyone: improving the quality of the product we were producing. However, the highest paid job in the plant turned out to be the repair people who fixed the defective product. They naturally assumed that if the quality improved, there would be fewer repairs required and the employees making repairs would be out of a job. When it was discovered how upset the workers were, the leaders eventually made a commitment that everyone would have a job and that no one's pay rate would be reduced. When the quality did improve and there were far fewer repairs needed, the leaders kept their word and found homes for all of the repair workers and did not change their pay rates. This created trust between the leaders and the employees and they were eventually able to achieve great improvements.

The Style 3 – Team Forming Leader understands that to get to true collaboration, it is critically important for the entire organization to trust each other, work well together, not blame others for failures driven by defective processes, and create a culture based on teamwork. If the Style 3 leader is truly engaged in making this significant culture change, then they will go through all of the same training as their employees (not executive overviews but the full classes), serve on an improvement team as a participant on a regular basis, and fill the sponsor role for other improvement teams. Several organizations that have gone down this path now require that every employee, including the CEO and every other leader, serve at least one week a year on an improvement team. When an organization is able to achieve this level of commitment to teamwork, the path to achieving excellence begins to materialize.

8

Flexing Back to Style One
Crisis Leader

*Amazing leaders know how to "flex" styles depending
on the current needs of the organization*

THE STORY OF JIM BROWN

Things were finally showing signs of turning a corner for Jim Brown and
his division of JED, Inc. Six months had passed since Jim met Officer
Joe Brittain in that dark parking lot on his first day in his role as Vice
President. He still parked his old Ford truck in the back of the employee
lot and once or twice a week made sure to stop by Joe's security booth to
have a quick cup of coffee before starting his day. He would also greet
employees as they walked into work and routinely ask them how things
were going and if there was anything he could do to help. This went a long
way toward creating an open, inviting culture. About half of the employees
had now been through "team and process improvement" training and
a little over a third were serving on a dozen employee teams that were
working on a multitude of problems and improvement ideas. Momentum
was slowly beginning to show signs of improvement and the key metrics
were all going in the right direction. However, even though these metrics
were improving, some were not yet up to where they were before Jim tore
up the old quality reports (Figure 8.1).

Jim was especially pleased with the safety audit scores as they got closer
to 100%. David and the facilities workers, as well as several teams of
employees, had done an outstanding job of cleaning up huge portions of
the office and production areas. They worked hard to paint and organize

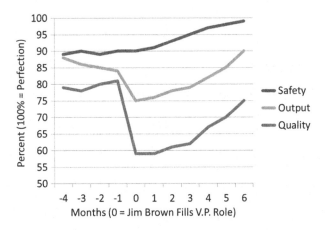

FIGURE 8.1
Key Performance Metrics.

each area and install the new, energy-efficient lights. The building had been transformed from a dark, dirty dungeon to a bright, cheery place to work and these transformations, along with the safety improvements being driven by the audits, were having a positive impact on the safety metrics. It was also becoming clear that the employees embraced the new work areas and this was building a sense of pride within the workforce. Jim finally felt comfortable inviting customers to visit the facilities to showcase the teams' progress and improvement efforts.

Another indicator that things were heading in the right direction was the customer satisfaction number. The improvements that were made in the customer call center, along with the problem-solving teams' actions, contributed to the overall enhancement of the customer experience. Mary continued to meet with the customer representatives team and they had implemented a number of additional ideas that brought the average hold times down to a few seconds. In fact, the call takers had to change their standard greetings from "I am so sorry for your long wait on hold, how can I help you?" to "Thank you for calling the JED company, how can I help?" These calls went much better with the almost non-existent hold times, and the customer reps were thrilled with the results (Figure 8.2).

At one of their weekly staff meetings, Jim and his leadership team were going through the company performance reports when unexpectedly, Judy White, Jim's administrative assistant, opened the door and instantly gained everyone's attention. "Excuse me for the interruption," said Judy, "but this is critically important. Wayne Green is on the phone and I think

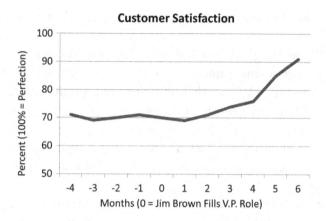

FIGURE 8.2
Customer Satisfaction Metric.

you might want to put him on the speakerphone." Everyone instantly knew the name Wayne Green as being the CEO of their largest customer.

Jim hit the button on the speakerphone and greeted Wayne and explained who was in the room listening in on their conversation.

"Thanks for taking my call," began Wayne. "We could really use your help with a significant crisis. Last night, a heater unit in one of our warehouses overheated and started a fire. Emergency personnel were on the scene within minutes and the fire was quickly extinguished and, thank God, no one was hurt. However, there was extensive heat, smoke, and water damage done to a small area which just happened to contain the entire amount of product we bought from you last month. Everything is ruined. Of course, we have insurance to cover the costs but we also have many customers who need this product and they are counting on getting their shipments. I know this will be a tough challenge, but is there any way we can get an emergency order in to replace what was destroyed?"

"I am glad to hear that no one was hurt in your fire, Wayne, and you have my word that we will do whatever we can to replace that product," replied Jim. "Please send me a list of everything you need and it would help to put the list in an order of priority. I will ask my leadership team to immediately begin to put a plan together to determine what it will take to coordinate our suppliers and internal resources in order to make this happen. We will give you a call in a couple of hours with our plan."

"Thank you so much for your help on this," replied Wayne. "This has the potential of doing great damage between us and our customer base, so anything you all can do to help will be welcomed and I will be eternally grateful."

After Wayne hung up, Jim instantly switched into crisis leadership mode. He went to the whiteboard and began to list all of the steps required to put the plan together and doled out assignments to each of the leaders. "Prepare for this to be a long month of many late nights," said Jim. "However, this is our chance to shine and solidify our relationship with our biggest customer. We will need to put everything else on hold, even the employee improvement team meetings until we manage our way through this crisis."

"Dang it," said David. "And just when we were starting to make some real progress. It is going to be tough to get things back on track."

"Hmmm…" thought Jim out loud. "You may be right. I need to make it clear what is going on and enlist the support of our entire workforce to help us through this crisis. Also, I will reassure everyone that this is a temporary change and we will get back to the training and team meetings as soon as possible. Let's get all of our employees together and I will share with them the urgency of this situation."

It took about 15 minutes to get everyone together in the parking lot and, just like 6 months prior, Jim climbed a ladder with a bullhorn in his hand. He asked David to record a video of the event on his phone.

"We need your help," he began. "Our largest customer who has been doing business with us for decades is in trouble and has asked us to provide whatever assistance we can. Last night, their warehouse caught fire and in the process of putting out the flames, the area that stores the products they buy from us was severely damaged. Some of the units in the shipment were lightly damaged and they are going to send those back to us for repair and complete refurbishment. The rest, we will need to replace with new products. This additional demand will far exceed our capacity, so we will need to work as many hours as possible. Next weekend is a holiday and I know some of you already have vacation plans with your families. Please, keep those plans. Family is important. For the rest, if there is any way possible to put your celebrations on hold and come into work, our customers will be grateful and our leadership team and I will be in your debt."

One of the employees in the back of the group yelled, "I will be here to help!" This was soon followed by several other employees yelling, "We've got your back!" and, "You can count on us!" The entire group erupted in applause and sounds of "Whoop! Whoop!" could be heard as the pride of the moment began to swell. Jim was visibly moved as he began to realize that this group of employees was finally coming together as a cohesive team.

After the enthusiasm died down, Jim picked back up the bullhorn and began again. "Thank you for your enthusiastic support. This is going to be a tough few weeks but I know we can pull through. Unfortunately, we will need to put everything on the back burner until we are able to get back on our feet. So, we will be postponing the training and team meetings but you have my word that we will begin all of this again next month. We have come a long way and I want to make sure we do not lose momentum. Please feel free to continue discussing ways we might improve our processes while working on the production lines and during your shift start-up meetings. My hope would be that when we reschedule the team meetings next month, each of you will be prepared to share some new ideas on how we might improve."

All of a sudden, Judy, Jim's administrative assistant, came running up to the ladder with her cellphone in her hand. When she caught Jim's attention, she blurted out loud enough to be picked up by the bullhorn, "Your wife is on the phone. She just went into labor! She said you need to get to the hospital right away! You all are about to have a baby!"

The crowd erupted in applause again with shouts of congratulations. Susan, the director of operations walked up to the ladder and took the bullhorn away from the stunned Jim Brown. She yelled to the crowd, "Go Jim! We won't let you down! We will take care of things here and you go be with your wife and family!" The crowd again erupted in applause and parted to provide a path so he could get to his truck and leave the parking lot.

Jim was overwhelmed with emotion as he climbed down the ladder, thanked everyone, and ran to his old pickup truck and drove out of the parking lot. He was able to get to the hospital just in time to be there for the birth of their healthy, six-pound, seven-ounce baby daughter.

The next month was a significant challenge for Jim both at home and at work but everyone rallied around the need to satisfy their customers. One morning, after they finished the last of the emergency order for Wayne Green's company, Jim walked into his office and a giant Teddy Bear was waiting for him with a note. "I saw the video of your speech with your employees. You have a fine group of people working there at JED, Inc., and I am truly grateful for all of your help. Please pass along my thanks and congratulations for a job well done! P.S. Congratulations to you and your wife as well. We showed the video to our entire workforce and they chipped in to buy this gift for your new baby girl. Best wishes. Wayne Green"

THE STORY OF FRANK SMITH

At the same time Jim was reading his note of thanks, a new development was occurring within the other division of JED, Inc. Frank Smith could not believe the good fortune that had just fallen into his lap. He could barely comprehend what he was hearing from Bill, his director of quality. His peer and rival, Jim Brown, had called when Frank was out to lunch and, since it was urgent, the receptionist routed it to Bill. "Can you run this by me again to make sure I heard you right?" asked Frank.

"Jim Brown needs our help," explained Bill. "They have been working a ton of overtime lately trying to fill a major order and they are running low on several raw materials and he wanted to know if we had some of these materials to spare."

"Do we have what he is looking for?" asked Frank.

"Yes, for the most part, we have enough material in our inventory to meet our needs and theirs. Do you want me to pull the parts he is asking about and send them on our next truck?"

"Are you crazy? No way!" replied Frank. "We need every screw and bolt and pellet of plastic and have nothing extra to spare. Jim will have to find another way to dig himself out of this hole he has created for himself."

"But, I don't understand," said Bill. "We are all part of the same company. Don't you want to help?"

"You are such an idiot when it comes to how things work in the real world," said Frank with a bit of smugness. "The boss that Jim and I report to is close to retirement and in poor health. Any day now, he could decide to leave and there is a good chance that either Jim or I will be promoted into that position. For your sake, you better do everything you can to make sure I get that promotion. You have a lot of skeletons in your closet. Only a few of us know how we really got better quality numbers and I don't think you will want that information to leak out to the rest of the company."

Bill's face turned beet red and he slumped in his chair as he realized that Frank was right. "What do you want me to tell Mr. Brown about our inventory? If he wanted, he could pull up the corporate reports and see that we have the material he is looking for."

"I am so tired of being the only one around here with all of the answers," said Frank. "Look, just put a quarantine on all of our inventory. Say that it all failed inspection and is now on hold. That will take the material out of the inventory reports that show it is available. When we need the material for our own use, we will move the parts out of quarantine and, then like magic, it will show up on the books. This is a simple trick to hide inventory when we want to make our metrics look better. That is how we have been able to show significant improvement in our inventory numbers in order to achieve excellence. Learn from the master."

"I was wondering how we were able to show such a huge decrease in inventory when it appears that every shelf is as full as ever," replied Bill. "I guess this is what it takes to get ahead and recognized by upper management."

After Bill left with his marching orders, Frank sat back in his chair and smiled. "It feels good to mentor the next generation of managers in this company," he thought to himself. "Bill did bring me a nice gift, so I guess sharing a bit of my wisdom is the least I could do. Now, what to do with this information about Jim Brown's division struggling to find enough material to keep things going? Hmmm… I have an idea."

Frank turned on his computer and began crafting a letter. "To Whom It May Concern, I represent a major customer of the JED, Inc. and feel that my needs are no longer being met. I wish to remain anonymous so there will be no retribution. My order delivery dates have extended well beyond what is acceptable. I called your Vice President, Jim Brown, and was told that they are running out of supplies and to be patient. This sounds like mismanagement to me. Please look into these problems and try to have them fixed before my next order or I will be forced to find a new supplier. Thank you for your consideration. A friend and customer of JED, Inc."

Frank printed out the paper and put it into an express shipment envelope in order to hide the origin of where the letter was sent from and addressed it to the JED, Inc. corporate office. "Someone has to make sure the boss knows what is going on around here," he thought as he dropped the letter into the local mailbox with a smile.

PRACTICAL APPLICATIONS

The story in this chapter introduces two concepts: the need for leaders to flex their leadership style depending on the organization's current needs and some of the benefits associated with going down the path of achieving employee collaboration.

FLEXING LEADERSHIP STYLES

Circumstances both outside and within an organization are constantly in flux. An effective leader will know when it is appropriate to change his or her leadership style to match what is required at any given point in time. This, of course, requires several factors to be in place in order for this to happen.

- First, the leader will need to fully understand the four styles of leadership we have discussed (Crisis Leader, Idea Gathering Leader, Team Forming Leader, and Empowerment Leader). They will need to understand the benefits of each and feel comfortable fulfilling the role required to be successful in each style.
- Next, the leader will want to be aware of what is going on throughout the organization, with their suppliers and with their customers, and flex to a different style if the situation requires this adjustment. For example, if a true crisis occurs, then the leader will need to quickly assess the situation and make the shift to Style 1 – Crisis Leadership in order to do whatever is required to right the ship and navigate through the current set of issues. Another situation that could trigger a need to flex would be if a team becomes dysfunctional. The leader may need to step in and demonstrate Style 2 – The Idea Gathering Leader and begin making the tough decisions after listening to all of the recommendations from the team.
- The leader will then shift, temporarily, to this new way of leading. This requires substantial communication and a strong commitment on the part of the leader to move as quickly as possible back to the path of progressing toward collaboration. It is important that the organization understand that there is a need for the leader to temporarily take control. Trust can be lost if the employees think that there really isn't a crisis and that the leader is using these current circumstances to regain power and move back into an old-style manager role.

Just like Jim Brown did in the story, it is important to communicate the current situation and explain when and how things will get back on track in order to continue moving the organization toward teamwork and collaboration. If this is done in the correct way, there is a fairly high probability that the employees will rise to the occasion and go above and beyond to help the leaders get through the current situation.

COLLABORATION BENEFITS

Why bother going through the difficult transformation to change the culture of an organization? Why take the time and spend the resources needed to make improvement happen? Why implement teams and strive to achieve collaboration? Below are some of the possible answers to these questions:

In order to cut costs – If this is your answer to the questions above, then you will be sorely disappointed in the results of any improvement effort and will be on the road to failure. As was mentioned in the last chapter, reducing tangible, measurable costs can be difficult. The three main cost reductions that most accountants would agree are real savings include: reducing labor costs, reducing material costs, and reducing overhead costs. If the improvement efforts eliminate labor, then the teams will eventually fail and the employees will be bitter and despise the leaders and the organization (See *Don't Do Stupid Stuff!* in the previous chapter). As far as material is concerned, the main cost is the price of incoming parts, and most employees outside of purchasing will not have much impact on prices. Overhead costs are usually controlled by the leaders and may be reduced through greater productivity (more units produced = less overhead per unit). This will only happen if there is demand for more products or services and the teams, outside of sales, may not have much control over this happening. If cutting costs are the focus, developing leaders and teams is not a priority and the ability to achieve excellence will be difficult if not impossible. However, achieving team collaboration and a focus on excellence will lead to more demand, extra capacity, and productivity gains that will eventually lead to greater profits. The organization's executives need to look at all of this as an investment that will pay handsomely down the road.

In order to delight the customer – This is getting closer to the mark. Customers in whatever form (patients, constituents, patrons, etc.) are the lifeblood of all organizations. Keeping them satisfied and even delighted is critical to the long-term success which will lead to job security, investment returns, and growth. Since customer's expectations are constantly changing, performance by the organization that might have been satisfactory in the past may not come close to meeting customer requirements today. If the organization is not constantly improving its processes, designs, quality, etc., then it is on a path of destruction and may not be aware of its fate until it is too late. There are many examples of organizations that were considered to be examples of excellence and then quickly went out of business due to their inability to keep up with the changes in their customers' expectations.

Another factor to consider when discussing meeting the needs of the customer is how well the competition meets these same needs. In the past, customers had a certain degree of loyalty to the organizations that provided them with products and services. In many cases, that is no longer true. Every organization must win over the customer with each order, call, and interaction. With social media, instant reviews, and good old-fashioned word of mouth, the perception of customer satisfaction can change quickly. And, if enough bad publicity seeps into the public's consciousness, they will switch to a competitor. It is critically important that the entire organization figures out how to work together, develop the best products and services, and have predictable processes with sufficient capacity to meet demands… all of this done at a reasonable price with terrific quality and fast delivery. This can only be achieved if the entire organization has migrated to the collaborative side of the Leadership Progression Model.

In order to inspire your employees to achieve excellence – Bullseye! I would wager that if 100 improvement professionals were asked why they are so dedicated to making team-based, continuous improvement happen, some form of the words "inspiration," "ownership," and "satisfaction" would be part of their answer. I have been in the improvement field for most of my career and can tell you from experience that there is no greater feeling of accomplishment than seeing an entire organization of people transform from a group of hateful, spiteful, zombie-like creatures to one of excitement, fulfillment, support, trust, collaboration, and accomplishment. People spend a significant portion of their lives at work and yes, a small number just want a paycheck. But my experience is that most want to be challenged, want to feel like they are making a difference, want to be heard, want to feel a sense of accomplishment, and want to be part of a winning team.

What does all of this goodwill with the employees buy an organization? The financial community will have a difficult time calculating a Return on Investment for teamwork and improving processes. However, there are many, many tangible and intangible benefits that can be realized.

TANGIBLE BENEFITS

Predictable Processes – When employee teams work to improve their processes by eliminating waste, eradicating errors, and understanding and reducing variation, these processes become much more predictable. In one business, when it launched its improvement initiatives, it was making roughly 1,300 units a day, ±1000! Some days were awful and everything went wrong and they barely made 300 units. The very next day, things might go perfectly and they would produce over 2,200 units. The employees (and managers) had no idea how things would go from day to day. This made planning and communicating with suppliers and customers almost impossible. Three years later, after migrating to collaborative teams of employees working together to improve their processes, they were making roughly 2,300 units a day, ±1. It did not matter if this was the beginning or the end of the quarter, the Friday before a holiday weekend, or any other day, they could count on 2,300 units being produced. This made it significantly easier to hit promise ship dates with their customers and submit predictable orders to their suppliers.

Having predictable processes is important for all types of organizations. If a company is a job shop with significant variability in their customer demands, plans can still be made based on predictable times for each, individual step required to get a specific job done. For service organizations, having predictable processes for executable tasks will develop a foundation that will allow the service providers to have confidence that when they are asked by their customer for help with something, they know that a response to that request will happen a certain way and within a certain amount of time. The anxiety level within the entire organization is greatly reduced when processes become well understood and predictable.

Understanding Capacity – Customers (internal and external) place demands on your processes and every process has a certain amount of capacity. If there is a great deal of variation in these processes, it becomes difficult to know if there is enough overall capacity to meet the demand of the customers. This uncertainty places employees into a position where they are required to guess when things will get done and, in many cases, they get it wrong. This makes the customers think that the employees are either ill-informed or that they are content with outright lying when their needs are not met. However, when processes become more predictable, it is easier to compare capacity with customer demands. If demand is over capacity, then the employee teams can work to try and break bottlenecks in order to provide additional output. If demand is less than capacity, then the marketing and sales organizations can develop plans to sell more products or services. Producing more with the same number of employees and the same overhead costs is one way organizations can significantly improve their profit margins.

For service organizations, having predictable processes reduces the uncertainty of what might happen, and fewer fires will need to be dealt with. This means that the employees (or volunteers in a non-profit) can spend more of their time working with the people they are helping (increased capacity). This allows the service organization to provide more offerings and help more people. For example, in one non-profit organization, when it was working with several broken processes, it could only handle 150 children with 100 adult volunteers in a summer program it offered. The leaders of this group formed several teams and redesigned many of the processes, and the same 100 adult volunteers now work with over 350 children and everyone is happier and more fulfilled.

Reduction in Reserves – Every error made in a process adds to the overall cost of the organization. These costs may consist of damaged material, wasted resources, and lower demand as customers become frustrated. As employee teams work together to solve problems by developing robust, predictable processes, overall costs associated with errors and waste will come down. Most organizations set up accounting reserves to cover these costs. At the end of the year, these reserves will have significant amounts of funds left over that can go directly to the bottom-line.

Inventory is another form of reserves. Predictable processes will reduce the need to keep "just in case" inventory on hand… just in case something goes wrong, there is a backup supply. Again, as processes become more predictable, the need to hold onto unnecessary inventory is lessened. Reducing inventory will free up cash, clear out space that can now be utilized for value-added operations, and lessen the chance that parts will be lost or damaged.

INTANGIBLE BENEFITS

Enthusiastic Productivity – Have you ever participated in a champagne spraying moment at work? Every time a sports team wins the big game, they go back to their locker room, put on safety glasses, and then pop open several bottles of champagne and spray it all over themselves, their teammates, and their coaches. Their excitement at winning the championship game cannot be contained. They celebrate the accomplishments of the entire team after a long season of collaboration that includes working together to analyze game film, practice plays over and over to get them just right, building endurance and strength in the weight room, and working with their coaches to maximize the output of the entire team. Champion-caliber teams do not have superstars playing at every position; in fact, in some cases, sports analysts will point out that most of the players may be really good but not necessarily great. Yet, they continue to win. This is driven by "enthusiastic productivity."

In the old management ways of the last several decades, the belief was that the only way to get more productivity from workers was to use fear. Fear of losing a job, fear of not getting a raise, fear of being forced to work overtime, fear of doing a job that no one else wanted to do, etc. Fear will motivate workers for a short period of time, which will artificially increase productivity. However, fear also burns people out and they will eventually do one of two things: find another job or get to the point where they just don't care and do the bare minimum to get by. There might be a short-term burst of productivity but, in the long run, overall efficiency suffers. When this happens, old-time managers will use even greater doses of fear, which might include yelling at and demeaning the employees. This creates a toxic work environment, which eventually leads to the employees becoming examples of the walking dead that Jim encountered in Chapter 1. It does not need to be this way.

Employees, who have the opportunity to collaborate on a team, may not spray each other with champagne, but they will work hard to help their organization be successful. I have witnessed large groups of people go way beyond what was expected of them to get a major order finished, make significant process improvements, do whatever they can to help make sure that their customers' needs are being met, and flawlessly launch a new product or service. When employees are treated with respect, strong communication practices are put into place, and they can see their ideas for improvement being implemented, their sense of pride and ownership begins to swell and "enthusiastic productivity" begins to naturally happen.

When a crisis hits like it did with Jim Brown's part of the business in the story portion of this chapter, if the culture has reached Style 3 or 4 Leadership on the Progression scale, employees will rally around the leaders and most will do whatever they can to help the organization succeed. It is impossible to put a cost-to-benefit calculation together to capture how this impacts the bottom line, but it will show up in several of the key metrics including customer satisfaction.

One other note about the benefits of experiencing "enthusiastic productivity": as word spreads about the positives associated with working in an empowered team environment, people will begin to take notice and want to work for these organizations. This gives the leaders the opportunity to select the best candidates to fill open positions. For example, one organization migrated to Style 3 and 4 leadership throughout and the next time they had an open position, candidates lined up for blocks in order to get on the interview schedule. This had never happened before. Several of these candidates said that they were there purely due to the fact that they had heard from their family and friends how great of a place it was to work. From that point forward, they had a long waiting list of people who wanted to be a part of the teams.

Value-Added Suppliers – For decades, most organizations treated their suppliers as the enemy (or with a great deal of disdain). However, any supply chain is only as strong as the weakest link. If that weak link is with a supplier, then the process will eventually break down and customer satisfaction will suffer. When an organization moves toward collaboration, they will begin to view their suppliers in a different light. I have worked with several teams that regularly included representatives from those organizations' suppliers. They provided tremendous insight as to how portions of the process work that might be hidden from the employees and usually provide powerful ideas on how to improve.

For example, in one company that produced large, heavy, machined parts, the supplier welded metal blocks to the parts in order to move them through their part of the process. Their last step was to remove these blocks and spend a considerable amount of time and resources to grind the welds down to a smooth surface. When these heavy parts arrived at the plant that ordered them, the first step in their receiving process was to weld similar metal blocks to the parts in order to move them through their factory. When this was uncovered in a team meeting, an agreement was made to leave the blocks in place throughout the process. This resulted in significant cost savings that was shared between the supplier and the company.

Also, when processes become more predictable, suppliers are able to better plan for the demand placed on their own capacity. This allows for more predictable ship dates and even better quality since suppliers will be less likely to rush orders through their part of the process.

Able to Accept Change – When I was on a 2-year assignment at General Electric to go around and collect best practices from organizations who were achieving excellence, one of the things that stood out was the fact that companies that were already doing well with their improvement efforts had a culture that embraced change. In fact, several of the employees I spoke with indicated that, to them, change meant improvement and growth. If change slowed down or stopped, they began to worry that maybe the company was beginning to become stagnant, which could ultimately put their jobs at risk. This is a departure from the way most employees think about change.

People usually like to stay in their comfort zones. This creates a natural resistance to change. To demonstrate this fact in my workshops, I ask participants to cross their arms. I then ask them to re-cross their arms but this time, take the arm that was on top and put it on the bottom (give it a try). After about 5 seconds, I tell the group that they can stop. Almost immediately, most of the participants drop their arms or go back to the original way. When I ask them why they changed back to the original stacking of their arms so quickly, they will share with me that the second attempt felt uncomfortable and they wanted to get back to the way that felt best to them. This phenomenon can occur when trying to improve (change) a process.

If your organization is able to overcome their fear of change, this will open the doors to making improvements happen on a regular basis. Also, as customer needs change and new products and services are introduced, the work teams will take it all in stride and help make the modifications happen instead of providing a constant barrier. If your organization can achieve this level of employee support and involvement, this will become a significant benefit that will be difficult to quantify.

These are just a few examples of the benefits associated with organizations that have achieved collaboration and teamwork with their employees. In the next chapter, several additional benefits will be discussed.

9

Style Four Leadership – Empowerment Leader

Saying that teams are empowered is much easier than actually empowering them

THE STORY OF JIM BROWN

"Before we start our leadership team meeting," began Jim Brown as he addressed his staff. "I have a video I would like to share." Jim turned on a TV monitor and the screen showed the image of a baby girl hovering over a cake with one lit candle. In the background several people were singing "Happy Birthday." The girl began to blow and spit in order to put out the candle. Finally, a couple of adults bent down and helped her finish the job with great fanfare. In fact, the adults were so thrilled with this accomplishment, they failed to notice the little girl pick up a handful of cake and icing and smear it all over her face. This of course thrilled the little girl and caused peals of laughter within the gathering.

Jim's leadership team also broke out in laughter and then applause. It had been one year since that day when he had to rush to the hospital and what a year it had been. All of the employees had now been through "team and process improvement" training with almost half of them going through a second round of more advanced training. Over 50 team events had now taken place with significant improvements to the stability and efficiency of the various processes. They continued to do the safety audits and had achieved 100% compliance for the past seven months. The employees welcomed the safer work environment with many thanking Jim and the other leaders for caring about their well-being. The focus on safety continued and teams were now being challenged to look for ways to redesign the various process steps to prevent repetitive injuries, backaches, and other muscle strains that could cause short- and long-term health problems. Jim had even gotten approval to build a small employee gym on-site to promote better health practices.

The quality scores had also improved significantly and were now consistently over 97%, which was better than when Jim started, but still far from perfect. Also, the improvements resulted in more stable processes and the production folks were able to more accurately commit to when products would be shipped so their "on time" delivery scores were getting better. Customer satisfaction, which took a small hit for a few months after they focused on getting Wayne Green's emergency order done, had now climbed back to the high 90% range.

Everyone agreed that there had also been a significant improvement in the morale of the workforce. People were actually beginning to look forward to coming to work. Occasionally, laughter could be heard over the noise of the machines indicating a feeling of mirth that was replacing the old feelings of fear. To show his appreciation for all of the hard work and improvements that had been realized, Jim and the leadership team hosted several events including a celebration day. One Saturday, everyone was invited to bring their families and guests to enjoy a carnival that had been set up in the employee parking lot. During this day of fun, good food, and music, Mary Robinson, the production worker who helped start the process of sharing improvement ideas, had the opportunity to introduce her husband to Jim, his wife Danielle, and their new baby girl. They spent quite a bit of time during the catered lunch discussing the finer techniques of fly fishing and swapping stories about raising a new baby.

"It has been quite the year," said Jim to his staff as he changed the TV monitor image to one showing the latest round of monthly metrics. "We have certainly made a lot of progress but we still have a ways to go to get even close to achieving excellence. However, each day, I become more and more confident that we are on the right path to achieving our vision and mission. I think we are ready to take the next step on our journey."

"Our next step?" asked David, the leader of facilities. "I thought we were getting pretty close to being done with making changes."

"The moment we are done making changes," replied Jim. "Is the day we file for bankruptcy and close this business down. No, we must keep pushing ourselves and not become complacent. I got word the other day from our sales and marketing teams that our competitors have gotten wind of the improvements we are making and that they are all starting to get worried. One of them has now launched their own improvement efforts and I have heard that they even tried to hire away a couple of our best workers. Fortunately, both employees are happy with our approach here and turned them down. That is another piece of evidence that we are on the right track."

"What is this next step you mentioned?" asked David.

"We have been utilizing our employee problem solving and process improvement teams now for almost a year and have made significant progress with the training. I think it is time to plan and implement our first fully empowered employee team."

"Whoa... wait a minute," exclaimed Susan Jones, the leader of operations. "What does that mean exactly? Are you actually suggesting that teams of our employees are going to run parts of the business? I admit that I was wrong when it came to asking our employees for their ideas and putting teams together to solve problems and make improvements. But... I don't know if I am okay with actually allowing people outside of this room to make business decisions."

"Our employees make a multitude of decisions that impact our customers every day," replied Jim. "What I am proposing is not that earth-shattering. Let me walk you through my thoughts on this and then I would like each of you to think about this proposal and come back to our next staff meeting with your recommendations and concerns. Once we can all reach consensus on a plan, we will pick a small part of the business to try the changes and see how they work. If everyone is comfortable that this first empowered team is working, we will begin to try this new model in other areas. You have my word that we will only progress as fast as this group is comfortable. However, I do feel that this is a critical step needed to achieve real excellence."

"Alright," said Susan. "Let's hear your proposal and then we can give it some thought. As far as a place to give this a try is concerned, I bet Mary Robinson's production line would be as good a place as any."

"Yes, I agree," said Jim. "This is my proposal..." Jim went over to the whiteboard and began to sketch a diagram of a new team structure (Figure 9.1).

"Once we have selected an area of our business to give this a try, I would like for us to identify all of the resources that support that particular part of the process. These resources will then become part of a dedicated team and will work together in order to make their system of processes the best

FIGURE 9.1
Proposed Team Structure.

it can be. In order for this to happen, all of these folks will be relocated so they can sit together and be near the production area they are supporting. Also, most of their goals and objectives will be based on how well they are able to work together as a team in order to meet their customers' needs. The rest will be individual goals focused on self-enrichment, mentoring and coaching others, and the part they play in helping their team be successful."

"Our job," continued Jim. "Will be to do what we can to support this team by giving them the tools and data they need in order to be successful as well as empower them to make the necessary decisions to meet their daily requirements. We will also need to do what we can to help them resolve problems and make continuous improvements to their processes." Jim paused for a minute to let this sink in. "So, what are your thoughts?"

The group's reaction to this idea ranged from confused to amused as they tried to comprehend what Jim had just told them. This concept was radically different from what this group of leaders was accustomed to, and the shock of it all was having an impact.

Susan was the first to speak. "Who would be the boss of the people on this team? I see you have a team leader in the middle, would they report to that person?"

"Each member would take their direction from their team leader as far as day-to-day responsibility. However, we will need to decide if their 'boss' would still be their department leader or the team leader. There are pros and cons for each. Either way, it will be critically important that everyone in this room is on the same page and has common goals so we do not put our people in a position of having to deal with conflicting messages and priorities."

"I don't have enough resources to dedicate one of my purchasing people to this team," said Linda Parks, the leader of the procurement department. "Do you want me to hire more people in order to dedicate someone to each of these teams?"

"No, not necessarily," replied Jim. "If one of your purchasing people buys materials for multiple teams, when we get to that point, we can ask them to sit with the team that consumes the majority of their time and then, when we start a second team, they can flex over and help them when needed. We can be smart about how these resources are utilized."

"I see you have one of my quality folks on the team," said the leader of the quality organization. "Won't this cause a problem as far as keeping quality separate and independent?"

"No," replied Jim. "Remember, the quality resources will still be connected to the quality organization. However, the big change will be that instead of just being seen as the 'traffic cop,' walking around to find quality problems and writing tickets to the offenders, we will ask them to be part of the solution as well. In other words, since they are now part of the team, we will ask them to not only focus on finding the problems, but then work with the rest of their teammates to help solve the problems."

"I see that you have one of my maintenance folks on your diagram," said David, the leader of facilities. "I know just the person who would jump at the chance to be a part of a team. She loves working on the equipment in Mary's area and does a great job of taking ownership. I think she would be thrilled to be able to be dedicated to one of the teams and really focus on what would be required to keep the processes running smoothly."

"Ah, you must be talking about Rose Roberts," said Jim. "Let's discuss how this might play out for Rose. What could we do as a leadership team to support and empower Rose in order to give her what she needs to be successful?"

"Well, I would start by making sure she was well-trained on all of the equipment in her area," replied David. "Also, I could introduce her to all of the machine reps so she can more easily contact them for customer support."

"We could help make it easier for Rose to buy replacement parts by issuing her a company credit card," said Linda from purchasing.

"I would be okay with that," replied the leader of finance. "As long as there were limits and David committed to overseeing and reconciling the monthly statements. We may want to go the direction of empowered teams, but we still need checks and balances to be in place."

"I think that is reasonable," said Jim. "I would challenge Rose to help create a spare parts list and set up storage lockers to house these spare parts at each of the machines she is overseeing. We will also need a robust preventative and predictive maintenance plan. I have met Rose several times and if she puts in the same dedication and care as she does in keeping her vintage Ford Mustang in tip-top shape, the machines in her area have a great chance of running as smoothly as ever."

The more that the leadership team discussed this possibility, the more excited they got about what this could do regarding achieving their vision of striving for excellence. They also knew that this had the potential of turning their employees' worlds upside down, as many of them would need to change where they sat, who they interacted with, and how they would deal with the increased amount of day-to-day responsibility.

"Give this some more thought," said Jim at the conclusion of their meeting. "Next week, let's work out the details and settle on who will be on this first team. My goal would be to have this group up and running by the end of the month. We will then check on their progress on a regular basis and in three months, we will decide if we want to start a second team or go back to the original way things were done." Everyone agreed to this plan and committed to giving this new way of doing things a try.

All of the people who were selected to be on this first team were asked if they would like to give this new opportunity a try. Amazingly, everyone who was asked agreed to participate. All of the employees involved were then brought together and went through a new set of training classes that were focused on how to work as a team, the best ways to make decisions, how to handle conflict, and an explanation of the types of decisions they would make and the decisions that would still be made by the leadership team. All of the team members were then co-located in an area that was within a few steps of the processes they supported. The leadership team did everything they could to help this new team feel comfortable with the move. Each employee was told that if at any point in this transition they wanted to opt out, all they needed to do was alert anyone on the leadership team and arrangements would be made to move them back to their original departmental job and someone else would be asked to take their place. Fortunately, everyone stuck with the team through the transition.

Things started well enough. However, 3 weeks into their existence, this new team and their leaders were put to the test. A borderline quality issue was discovered by one of the production team members and she decided to shut the production line down. Per their team guidelines, a group was quickly assembled that included the quality inspector and engineer. They decided that the quality issue was significant enough to halt production until a fix could be put into place. Susan Jones, the leader of operations marched into Jim Brown's office with this news.

"I hope you are happy," Susan blurted out. "We are going to miss our production numbers for today because your 'empowered' team decided to shut down a major production line over a minor quality issue. I knew this was a bad idea."

"Hold on Susan," Jim replied. "I know this is a change in how things are done, but we all agreed to give this empowered team a shot and we need to support their decisions unless they do something unethical or unsafe. This quality issue... have you seen the problem and more importantly, would our customer's perception of our product and company be negatively impacted?"

"Yes, I have seen the problem and I would say that it would be less than a 10% chance that the customer would even notice and most of those would probably not care."

"We have been stressing the importance of achieving excellence and what you just described does not meet that standard. Let's take a walk and observe if the employees come together as a team and how they respond to this problem."

Susan and Jim put on their safety glasses and went to the production line that was selected to be the pilot area for the empowered team. They saw a group of employees huddled around a whiteboard and the team leader was taking them through a set of tools to help identify the root cause of the quality problem. This analytical work helped them identify the problem and determine a short-term solution as well as a permanent fix. They quickly tried out their idea for a solution and then they observed that the quality problem went away. The team celebrated by applauding and giving each other high fives. They were able to get the production line going without shutting down any other area more than a few minutes. Susan looked at Jim, nodded her head and smiled as she realized the importance of what had just occurred.

THE STORY OF FRANK SMITH

Six months after Jim Brown's division launched their first empowered team, Frank Smith was told that he had to attend a meeting that was taking place in one of Jim's conference rooms. Frank decided to take his quality manager, Bill, along with him. This was the first time either man had set foot in the building of their sister division since Jim took the V.P. position 18 months prior. "Wow, their building and campus grounds look amazing," Bill said to Frank as they got out of their car. "Not a broken window or cigarette butt in sight."

"Bahhh, that does not mean anything," exclaimed Frank. "I bet they spend a ton of company money paying someone to keep things in good shape. What a waste! Maybe I will have to tell our boss about this gross misuse of company funds."

They walked into the main lobby and were greeted with a warm smile by the receptionist who quickly checked them in, gave them their badges, and went over the safety rules. "I run my own freaking business," said an irritated Frank. "I don't need to be lectured on safety rules!"

"I am so sorry," said the receptionist. "But this is part of the process that our safety team, which I am a member of, came up with to help make sure our numbers stay at 100%." Without missing a beat, she continued going over the rules and had each man sign a form that indicated that they understood and would commit to following their processes. She then issued them all of the personal protection equipment they would need for the day.

After their meeting, Jim invited Frank and Bill to go on a tour of their service call center, offices, and production areas. "Oh my!" exclaimed Bill as they entered the factory. "This place is amazingly clean, organized, and well-lit. I swear you could eat off of this floor."

"Humph," said Frank. "All cosmetics... None of this helps anyone meet a production deadline. Just a bunch of window dressing!"

"Actually," replied Jim. "Our employees do a great job of keeping things clean and organized. We routinely bring customers here and they tell us that our facilities are a great selling point. Plus, we can more easily spot leaks and other problems, which helps us keep our perfect safety record intact."

They walked into Mary's production area and Jim explained how they now had four empowered teams running day-to-day operations in four different parts of the business, including their newest team in the customer call center.

"Empowered teams?!?" responded Frank. "What a bunch of nonsense. I hope you are not implying that your employees are actually being allowed to make decisions and changes without four or five approvals and signatures? If that is what you are saying, then it sounds to me like you are trying to shirk your responsibilities as a manager. If there isn't someone who is exerting total control over these people, ruling them with an iron fist, there will be chaos."

At that precise moment, one of the massive machines on Mary Robinson's line shut down and several lights started flashing indicating a major failure had just occurred. "Aha!" exclaimed Frank. "I knew this was a bunch of bull. You have major machine failures just like the rest of us. I guess you can kiss your production targets and customer satisfaction metrics goodbye for today."

Amazingly, within a couple of minutes, a group had formed at the control panel of the machine. Rose, the maintenance person, took charge and demonstrated crisis leadership as she assigned actions to several two-person teams. One group that contained an electrician was asked to go check the circuit breakers, one group was asked to review the diagnostic printout from the machine, one group was asked to lockout the machine and check for any jammed parts, and one group was asked to check the preventive maintenance logs and fluid levels. The groups dispersed with the goal of coming back together in seven minutes to share whatever information they had uncovered. Jim continued the tour with Frank and Bill but made it a point to return to the failed machine before the groups reconvened.

The quick response teams came back together within the seven-minute timeframe. Based on all of their information, it was clear that one of the motors in the machine had failed. Rose had already set up a spare parts cabinet next to the machine which had a replacement motor. She had also put quick disconnects on all of the wires and quick release bolts were already installed just in case a failure like this occurred. It only took 4 minutes to change out the motor and another 2 minutes to get the machine restarted. The total downtime was less than 15 minutes.

The next thing that happened was even more impressive. Rose told the quick response teams that they needed to meet during lunch to try and determine why the motor had failed and to work up a plan to prevent this from happening again in the future. She even told the group that she had permission to pay for their lunch using her own company credit card.

"Wow!" said Bill with a bit too much excitement. "That was pretty spectacular. With a failure that massive, we would have been down for most of the day." Frank shot Bill a look that clearly indicated that he should shut his mouth!

"Bravo Jim," said Frank as he started slowly clapping. "Do you take us for fools? It is clear that you preplanned this little demonstration to make us think that you and your leaders are doing something special. Well, I am not buying any of this garbage. Bill, go grab our coats and pull the car around, we are heading home right now before Jim can share any more of his lies!"

The drive home was done in silence as Frank needed some time to cool down and think. Finally he said to Bill, "We have a massive problem on our hands. Jim Brown and his little teams of misfit employees are starting to make us look bad. This will not stand! I think it might be time to make a move in order to solidify my position in this company." With that, Frank closed his eyes and drifted off to sleep for the rest of the ride home. Bill could have sworn a rather evil looking grin formed on Frank's face as he slept.

PRACTICAL APPLICATIONS

In the story portion of this chapter, we get a glimpse of a Style 4 – Empowerment Leader at work. This is by far the most difficult, radical change required to fully achieve excellence. I have had the opportunity to help several organizations migrate to Style 4 leadership and after getting through the anxiety associated with such a massive change, most participants have told me that it was the greatest thing that had ever happened to improve their job satisfaction. In one case, we asked everyone to give this new way of doing things a six-month try. After the six-month trial was completed, we got input from all of the team members. Over 98% said that they would never want to go back to the old ways and felt better about their jobs and about the overall organization than they ever thought possible. In every single case where Style 4 leadership has taken root, the performance metrics improved by an order of magnitude, including in safety, quality, delivery, and customer satisfaction.

If the use of fully empowered teams has such a profound impact, why isn't every organization pursuing this approach? There are a multitude of reasons including: management's fear of giving up too much power, fear of managers being overlooked for promotional opportunities if the teams are getting credit for the work, fear that a team of employees will make a mistake, fear of employees not coming together as a team and doing what is right for the organization, fear of sharing knowledge, fear of not following standardized processes, and overall fear of changing 100 years of deeply ingrained, old-style management practices. Unfortunately, there are several examples of companies that have gone out of business or were greatly hurt by not overcoming these fears and settling for mediocracy while their competitors focused on achieving excellence.

HOW DOES AN ORGANIZATION ACHIEVE STYLE 4 LEADERSHIP?

First, keep in mind that most organizations must go through Leadership Styles 1 through 3 to build a solid foundation before attempting to go to Style 4. I have witnessed several failed attempts to achieve empowered teams by jumping directly to the collaborative side of the leadership progression. Without a solid foundation of gaining experience reacting quickly to a crisis (Style 1), developing critical thinking skills (Style 2), and team-based problem solving (Style 3) and the training and standardized, well-documented processes that go along with these efforts, empowered teams will flounder, make mistakes, and eventually fall apart (which may have been the outcome desired by managers who really did not want to change and were actually just creating a façade). Typically, it will take a year or two to build this foundation before the organization is ready to attempt using empowered teams.

Next, the organization's highest level executives need to understand and embrace what it takes to be successful in utilizing empowered teams. This may require a complete change in how people are measured and rewarded (see Chapter 3), allowing leaders to shift from being in total control to becoming more of a coach, mentor, and cheerleader, and permitting teams to fail and learn. A newly created, empowered team needs to be cultivated and allowed to grow just like a newly hired employee. It is pretty rare, when bringing on a new employee, to throw them directly into a difficult decision-making process on their first day. Usually, they are eased into the position. The same on-boarding process needs to be utilized when launching an empowered team.

Finally, the employee teams need to have guidelines on what they can decide for themselves and when it is appropriate to involve the organization's leaders. Remember, the teams are being tasked with dealing with day-to-day activities, helping to solve problems, and providing ideas on how to improve and then assisting in the implementation of these ideas. The leaders are still responsible for the overall functioning of the organization. However, with the use of empowered teams, the leaders will have more time to focus on interacting with customers, researching trends in their industry, setting the vision and strategy in order to achieve the mission, coaching and mentoring their teams, and developing celebrations when certain milestones are achieved.

WHAT IS THE BEST ORGANIZATIONAL STRUCTURE TO SUPPORT THE USE OF EMPOWERED TEAMS?

Turning Supervisors into Team Leaders – The simplest and least effective way to achieve empowered teams is to simply change the job description and title of the employees' supervisors to team leaders. The expectation is that somehow this type of change will magically create teams and that the old "supervisor" role will transform into something radically different. This is rarely the case. The only way to make this work would be to do a deep assessment of the original supervisors to determine if they have the characteristics and values required to be a successful team leader. Some of these folks may need to be reassigned to individual contributor type roles, some may need additional training, and some may already be prepared to shift into a team lead position. In order to make a clean start, it may be necessary to move the new team leaders into areas they were not overseeing before so that the teams and team leaders can learn and grow their abilities together.

Co-locating Resources with Common Goals: Another team-based organizational structure would be the one portrayed in the story portion of this chapter. This structure brings together all of the resources required to help the team be successful. These resources can then be co-located near the processes and teams that they support. There are two versions of this team structure that may be subtle in their appearance but can have a profound impact on the possible success of truly becoming empowered teams.

The organization depicted in Figure 9.2 indicates that the team members report into their individual departments and are only loosely connected as far as the overall team is concerned. If the departments have their own goals and objectives, this structure has little chance of success. The team members will have their own priorities that will pull them in different

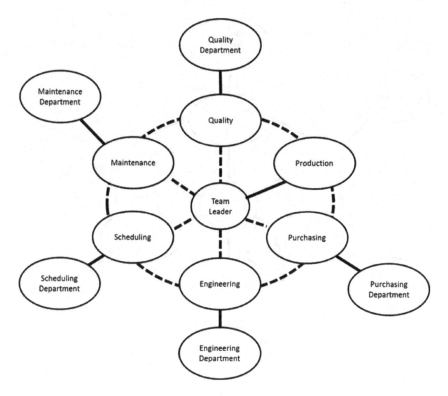

FIGURE 9.2
Team Members Report to Their Departments.

directions and chaos will reign. This will eventually cause the team to fracture and fail. Once this happens, the organization will probably slip back to the old style management philosophy.

Figure 9.3 shows that the employees are fully committed to meeting the needs of their team. The majority of their goals and objectives will be aligned and will focus on helping the team successfully meet the needs of their customers. The various departments become support teams to help provide information, best practices, and process guidelines. For example, the Engineering Support Team will set engineering drawing guidelines, testing procedures, and disposition of questionable quality for all of the engineers on each team. They would also pull all of the engineers together from time to time to help assure that all of these folks stay aligned in order to avoid sub-optimization.

One concern with this structure is the lack of independence of the quality organization. There may be an apprehension that the quality resources will become corrupted by wanting to support the success of their team

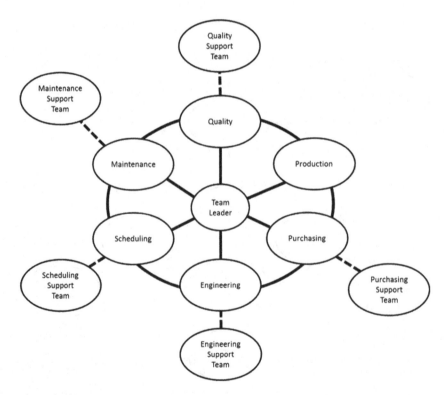

FIGURE 9.3
Departments Provide Support to the Team.

and purposely pass suspect product. The Quality Support Team can help address this by doing independent audits to make sure that the quality system is working. If this is not sufficient (military contracts usually require a completely independent quality inspection team for example), the next structure may be more appropriate.

Partnership of Process Design and Process Execution: This example is modeled after an organizational structure that I helped design during my time at General Electric and have used throughout my career with impressive results. This structure proved to be a solid conduit to assure improvement happens on a regular basis. It consists of two primary organizations to deal with the day-to-day fulfillment of products and services as well as dealing with problems and improvement opportunities. The two primary groups are known as the Order (or Service) Fulfillment Team (Process Execution) and the Process Innovation Team (Process Design) (Figure 9.4).

The Order Fulfillment Team (Process Execution) is similar to the co-located team with the exception of Quality and Engineering. These resources are consolidated in a new organization known as Process Innovation (Process Design). If you were to combine a Quality Engineer with a Manufacturing Engineer and an Industrial Engineer you would create a Process Innovation Leader. These folks wear all of these hats and are assigned to a specific part of the process and/or a specific Order Fulfillment Team. The Process Innovation Leader would need to partner with the Order Fulfillment Team Leader and together, along with all of their resources, they would be challenged to develop and execute a process that could meet all of the needs of their customers and help them achieve excellence.

The Process Innovation Leader is accountable for (with input from the workers) designing and improving all aspects of the process they are

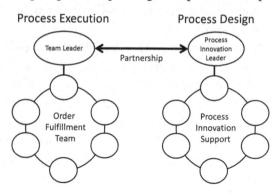

FIGURE 9.4
Process Execution and Process Design Team Structure.

responsible for. They seek out best practices from other organizations, research new technologies, work on quality concerns, and help drive the implementation of improvement ideas. Of course, all of this would not be possible without the input and ownership of the workers who are part of the Order Fulfillment Team. A good Process Innovation Leader knows that it is critically important to spend roughly half of their time walking the process, talking to the workers to determine where problems are occurring, and facilitating the gathering of ideas. The remaining 50% of their time can be spent working on projects, doing research, analyzing data, and making change happen to drive improvement. This 50–50 balance is important to maintain. If the Process Innovation Leader spends too much time walking the process, they could get pulled into the day-to-day fire-fighting that occurs when problems pop up and there will not be enough time to work on improving anything. If they spend less than 50% of their time walking the process and interacting with the workers, then the team will feel abandoned and will not buy into any of the improvements.

Since the Process Innovation Leaders are not full members of the Process Execution Team, they can meet the guidelines of quality systems that require independence from the resources that make quality decisions. However, in order for this to be successful, this group will need to feel as much accountability to meeting the needs of the customer as their partner group.

The Order Fulfillment Team would then take the process that has been designed and improved and do its best to follow the standard operating procedures and execute the process to the best of its ability. They would provide ongoing feedback to the Process Innovation Leader and participate in improvement idea generation meetings to continuously work on making things run smoother and more efficiently. The Order Fulfillment Team would share improvement goals to help solidify its partnership with the Process Innovation Team.

In order for this structure to work smoothly, there needs to be a true partnership between the Process Execution Team and the Process Design Team. This partnership will happen if each of the leaders has similar metrics, they pitch funding requests, improvement project ideas, personnel additions, etc. to the Executive Leadership Team together and they participate in the hiring and feedback process for each other's team members. Over time, the Order Fulfillment Leader and Process Innovation Leader will know each other's areas of responsibilities and they will be able to cover for each other when one of them is out of the office. Note: there may be a temptation to put both teams under the same leader. Don't go down this path. This will violate the desire to keep quality separate and will eventually lead to all of the Process Innovation folks being sucked into the day-to-day issues and the improvements will stop happening.

To help clarify the difference between these two groups, below are a few examples of what might occur and who would be responsible to take the lead in order to address these opportunities.

Safety Issue: The Process Innovation Leader is responsible to make sure that all processes are designed to be done in a safe manner. The Order Fulfillment Team is responsible for following all safety procedures. If an unsafe condition is discovered, the Order Fulfillment Team member would need to shut the process down immediately and get the Process Innovation Leader involved with assisting in the development and implementation of a corrective action.

Quality Issue: Similar to the safety concern, the Order Fulfillment Team member would need to shut down the process if a quality issue is discovered and immediately enlist the help of the Process Innovation Leader and Quality Support Team to develop a short-term and long-term corrective action. The Process Innovation Leader would take the lead, with assistance from Order Fulfillment, to design processes that reduce the risk of a quality issue occurring.

Equipment Failure: A maintenance person is assigned to look after a group of equipment by developing and executing preventive maintenance plans, setting up spare parts cabinets, as well as, in concert with the Process Innovation Leader, search for ways to make the equipment run smoother, faster, and longer. If a machine quits working, the first responder would be this dedicated maintenance person who would also lead the discussion about what went wrong and how to keep the failure from happening again.

A couple of notes about the Process Execution and Process Design organization model: some might think that going with this structure might take the emphasis away from utilizing teams of production workers (or those closest to doing the process) to make improvements happen. Actually, the opposite is true. In order to get buy-in and ownership with a process improvement, the Process Innovation Leader knows that they need to get the employees at all levels and in every department involved. Also, the number of ideas will increase substantially in these team meetings. I believe that the reason for this is that the employees know that the Process Innovation Leader will take the ideas, research the requirements and risks, and help get the improvements implemented (some employees are reluctant to share ideas because they think that they will be the ones who will be told to do all of the work to get them implemented). The Process Innovation Leader also has "skin in the game" since they are also being measured by how well the entire system does in meeting the needs of their customers. This provides an incentive to help make the processes as strong as possible, which requires buy-in from all of the workers.

An employee who has the opportunity to serve as a Team Leader on the Process Execution side for a few years and then has the opportunity to serve as a Process Innovation Leader on the Process Design side will have a solid foundation of experiences that should help this person as they move up the organization chart. In the companies that have implemented this structure, several have made it a requirement that future leaders have experience serving in each of these positions.

Finally, this structure is easy to scale up. Several organizations decided to give this new structure a try in one or two areas as a pilot. Then they would add another Process Innovation Leader when funds or headcount was freed up. Most of these organizations eventually covered every system, especially after they realized the many benefits. My experience is that the Process Innovation resources pay for themselves three to five times in the first year and five to seven times in the second year. This is a fantastic return on investment. In non-manufacturing organizations (health care, governments, non-profits, service), the concept is the same except the Process Innovation Leader may be a single resource instead of having a team of quality and engineering professionals.

These are just a few examples of ways to set up fully empowered teams for resources dedicated to meeting the needs of their customers and working together to achieve excellence. The empowered team approach also works with service providers, government groups, and non-profits. The names of the departments might be slightly different, but the concept is the same. In all cases, this is a huge step for any organization to take but the rewards are immense. The amount of goodwill, trust, ownership, and pride that will be developed by going down this route will create a significant amount of "enthusiastic productivity," which has the potential to propel the organization to heights it never dreamt possible. In the organizations I have worked with that were able to make this transition, words cannot describe the feelings of pride, accomplishment, and ownership that were realized by every participant.

10

The Unbroken Chain of Old Style Management

Rivers run deep and it is difficult to change the direction that the water flows

THE STORY OF JIM BROWN

20... 19... 18... 17...

Jim Brown and his leader of operations, Susan Jones, were standing on a balcony that overlooked the production factory. Susan invited Jim to witness something that had never happened before.

12... 11... 10... 9...

The empowered teams had been in place now for almost a full year and virtually every process had moved in this direction. Large electronic scoreboards were installed at strategic locations that displayed real-time data that indicated how they were performing in several key metrics. For the first time in the history of the JED Company, every display showed 100% for each of these metrics.

3... 2... 1... Ding! A chime sounded indicating that the workday was over.

"Woot!" exclaimed Susan as she gave Jim a slap on his back. "We did it! One hundred percent in every metric! This is amazing!"

Jim was about to reply when he put up his hand and said, "Wait a minute... do you hear that?"

They both listened intently. The noise started softly and began to grow louder. The employees, all throughout the business, were clapping! The enthusiasm of the clapping grew more intense with loud cheers joining the chorus. Jim looked at Susan and a big grin broke out. "This is amazing!" repeated Jim. "Not just the fact that we had our first day of 100% performance, but that the employees know that they were a big reason for this truly dramatic improvement. Their sense of pride, ownership, and empowerment has blossomed into spontaneous applause." At this point, the noise from the cheers was so loud that Jim could no longer be heard. Susan could have sworn that she saw a small tear of joy form in the corner of Jim's eye as the weight of this moment was making all of the challenges of the past 2 years worth every minute. Unfortunately, the celebration would be short lived.

The next day, Susan walked into Jim's office and told him that they needed to talk.

"Uh oh," said Jim. "It is never good news when someone walks in and says they need to talk. Did something bad happen in the factory? I was hoping our 100% performance would last longer than one day."

"No, we are still running well in the factory. Not quite a 100% performance today but we are over 99%. That is not what I wanted to talk about. I got some news this morning that I need to share. A company across town has heard about what we have done here and they asked me to come over and interview for a Vice President position in their organization. They called me this morning… and well… they gave me an offer I just can't refuse. I am sorry to have to say that I am turning in my notice."

"I would be lying if I said that I am surprised," said Jim. "From day one, I knew you were a V.P. caliber leader. We have been through a lot over these past couple of years and I know you are going to be great in this new role. I wish there was something I could say to get you to stay, but I would never want to rob you of a great opportunity. Please let me know if there is anything I can do to help in your transition."

"I remember that first staff meeting we had together," replied Susan. "I can remember thinking that you were one of the craziest bosses I have ever had. Well, I must admit that I was wrong. Thank you for teaching me what it is to be a true leader." Susan shook Jim's hand and left to go tell her team about this latest development.

Soon after Susan left, Jim's phone rang. "Hello, Jim Brown here. Yes, I can drive to the JED corporate headquarters. When do you want me there? Oh… you want me there today… as soon as possible. Sure, it sounds important. Let me clear my calendar. Since I am 3 hours away, I will try to be there by lunch."

Jim hung up the phone and thought, "Headquarters must have heard about our big 100% performance yesterday. I guess our CEO wants me to pass along his thanks to our employees. I better get on the road."

THE STORY OF FRANK SMITH

Things were moving quickly. Two weeks prior to Jim's 100% performance day, his counterpart, Frank Smith, began to implement his devious plan. Soon after a meeting Frank had with the boss he and Jim both worked for, he called a friend in the Corporate Human Resources department. "Hey, this is Frank," he told his buddy. "I was just in a meeting with my boss and it is my duty as a corporate officer to report a concern. As we both know, he is getting up in years and is close to retirement. Well, there is no doubt in my mind that my boss is in real trouble, health-wise. He was slurring his words, was so exhausted he could barely stand, and his face was red and he was perspiring uncontrollably." After a short pause as his friend responded, Frank said, "You say you saw him yesterday and he did not look like he was having any health problems. Well, maybe he had a mini-stroke last night. I am not a doctor, but I do know that he is not well... not well at all. It is Human Resources' responsibility to protect the integrity of the chain of command by looking into this concern. Okay, thanks for addressing this." Frank hung up the phone and waited for his plan to take hold. He did not wait long.

The gears and cogs of the corporate machine usually turn slowly. However, when the CEO makes a decision and changes need to be made, it is amazing how fast the inner workings of a corporation spring to life. Frank's friend in Human Resources went to his boss, the Corporate President of Human Resources, who then went to his boss, the Chief Executive Officer of JED, Inc. They quickly put together a very attractive "golden parachute" retirement package for Frank and Jim's boss. Even though he was in perfect health, Frank's boss reached the conclusion that this was too good of an opportunity to pass on and decided to retire early with a sizeable nest egg. The CEO thought about promoting Jim Brown into this newly vacant position but he was concerned about the drop in Jim's metrics that occurred a year prior and he did not feel that he had demonstrated the types of managerial skills needed for such a big promotion. "I haven't heard one complaint from any of Jim's employees for over a year now. He must have gone soft," thought the CEO. Jim seemed to spend way too much of his time traveling around and talking to customers and working on things like strategy and values. "Why isn't he available to make the hard decisions and put out fires?" Also, Frank's numbers were equally as impressive, especially his quality metrics. And Frank seemed to be much more in control of things, a real manager's manager. The CEO then remembered that there was an anonymous letter sent by an angry customer who claimed that Jim Brown had mismanaged their account. "I don't think I can take a chance on someone who has so many unknowns," he thought. After a brief pause, he decided to give the promotion to Frank Smith.

Later that week, Frank was flown to the Corporate Headquarters and after several days of tense negotiations, he accepted the position of Divisional President. One of Frank's first acts as President was to promote Bill, his old quality manager into his previous Vice President position. "Bill is not really qualified," Frank thought, "but it is better to have someone in that position who has some dirty laundry which will keep him loyal to me." Next, he told Human Resources to call Jim Brown and tell him to get to the corporate building as fast as possible. This was the call Jim received just after hearing Susan's news about leaving the company. Several hours after this call was placed, Jim was escorted up to Frank's new office.

"Come in and have a seat," said Frank as he motioned Jim to a chair so he could get settled.

"Wait a minute," said Jim preferring to stand. "Why are you sitting at our boss's desk?" Jim glanced at the door and saw the name "Frank Smith – Divisional President" on the nameplate. "What is going on here?"

"Our boss had some health issues and our kind-hearted CEO decided to give him an early retirement package. He then promoted the best V.P. in this company to take over as President. I started in this position yesterday."

"Are you trying to tell me that you are my new boss?!?" Jim's face turned a deep red as the realization of what was happening hit him like a brick.

"Yes, I am your new boss… but not for long." Jim noticed two security guards standing at Frank's door. "You, Jim Brown are a horrible manager. You did not have control over your people and you spent way too much of your time trying to get other people to do your work. You coddled your employees and allowed them to run all over you."

Jim quickly figured out what was about to happen. "The people in my part of the organization are amazing at what they do and they would do anything to help our business successfully meet the needs of all of our customers. Our productivity numbers are through the roof and we just hit 100% in all of our metrics...."

Frank closed his eyes. He clearly was not interested in anything Jim Brown had to say. Finally, he slammed his fist down on his desk and shouted, "That is enough!!! I don't want to hear any more of your fantasies. We all know that the only way to get excellence is to use fear and intimidation. You pampered your people and focused on making them feel good. What a crock. That will never work. You have 5 hours to drive back to your office and clean out your desk. Your employment with JED, Inc. is now terminated! Officers, escort this worthless pile of trash out of my office!"

THE STORY OF MARY ROBINSON, PRODUCTION WORKER FOR JED, INC.

Mary sat at her workstation staring at the clock on the wall. She felt like her soul had been ripped out of her body and now she was sitting here, a lifeless shell of her former self. It was now a little over a month since she lost two of the best leaders she could possibly want to work for. Susan Jones announced her departure and then the very same day, Jim Brown was fired and escorted out of the building. Poor Officer Joe was on duty when the call came in to make sure Jim Brown cleaned out his office and leave the property as quickly as possible. Joe refused to participate in the removal of his friend and mentor and was also quickly fired and told to go home.

Frank Smith hand selected Jim's replacement. Mary could not remember the name of this new Vice President but everyone had gotten accustomed to referring to him as Frank Smith Jr. He immediately put a halt to all of the training and the use of empowered teams and went back to the old, silo departments with the traditional hierarchical organization structure. He gave his staff a week to come up with individual goals and objectives and then raised all of the goals by 50% with a declaration that if any were missed, they would be immediately terminated. David, the director of facilities only lasted three days under this new regime. He fought hard to keep the maintenance folks empowered and dedicated to specific areas... maybe a bit too hard. He was escorted out of the building soon after. In fact, over half of the old leaders had either quit or been fired and all of them were replaced with managers who ruled with fear and intimidation.

Mary tried to adapt to this new management style. She kept trying to tell herself that this new way of doing things was not so different than what she experienced before Jim Brown had shown up and implemented his team-based structure. She shook her head as she tried to unsuccessfully remove the memories of all of the good times she experienced over the past two years. "Dang it, Jim Brown," she muttered to herself. "Why did you have to show up here? Why did you show us all a new way to work together and get us to a point where we were all feeling so good about our progress and future, only to have it all ripped away?"

She let out a long sigh and stared at her empty workstation. It had been over an hour since any product had shown up for her to work on. All of the scoreboards that showed the real-time data about how things were running had been turned off. "I bet management turned off those signs since all of the metrics have tanked over the past couple of weeks and they are embarrassed." Mary continued to sit and stare. There wasn't much else she could do. The days grew long and quiet. None of her old team members were allowed to talk with each other. Her new supervisor told her to shut up when she tried to discuss an improvement idea. He said that the company paid her to work, not to think or talk and that he was in control and would make all of the decisions. "How do you expect me to get a promotion if you workers do any of the thinking?" he told them.

Mary once again glanced at the clock. Tick, Tick, Tick. This was her new reality: sitting here staring at the clock on the wall waiting for this disaster of a day, week, month, career to be over.

She blinked and felt a tear roll down her cheek as she closed her eyes and sighed.

PRACTICAL APPLICATIONS

One of the fondest memories in my career paralleled what Jim and Susan experienced at the beginning of this chapter. I had the privilege to work with an organization that had several collaborative leaders and helped them follow a path similar to the one portrayed by Jim Brown. Over a three-year time period, we were able to shift the business unit to Style 4 Leadership – Empowered Teams and promote a vision of achieving excellence. We trained every employee and the teams worked hard to improve their processes. They were able to shrink the delivery times from 12 weeks to 2 days and improved quality at the pack station from the mid-80% range to over 99%. The first day we hit 100% in all of our metrics (which included safety, quality, and schedule attainment) we also experienced loud, spontaneous applause welling up from all of the work teams. That will be a day I will never forget.

On the flip side, I have also encountered many examples over the years of organizations that started to go down a path of using empowered teams of well-trained employees to drive improvement and at some point on their journey, it all came crashing down. This usually happens when the executives, for a number of reasons (cost cutting, concern for the loss of control, lack of trust that the employees have the business's best interest in mind, etc.), decide to pull the plug. They may not directly stop the improvements but can do great damage by promoting and hiring the wrong types of leaders or even going so far as to hire old-style managers into key positions.

Why is this disastrous for the employees and the organization? I have heard some form of the following statement from several employees over the years: "I wish that I had never known what it was like to be a valued member of a team, to be listened to and trusted, to be respected and empowered because it hurts so badly when it is all ripped away!" When the culture shifts forward and then returns to the old ways, not only are the productivity gains erased, but in many cases, productivity drops below what it was before the improvements started.

It is truly a sad situation when one visits an organization that once had a successful improvement initiative that eventually died. On the walls are communication boards that are no longer used, charts of metrics that haven't been updated for months or years, idea generation stations that have gathered dust, labels that are peeling off of shelves that once designated where things should be stored, and red lights indicating something is wrong that are now ignored.

Why consider starting down the path of achieving excellence if failure causes so much pain and damage? The productivity gains achieved through employee ownership, pride, respect, and enthusiasm (enthusiastic productivity) are too great to ignore. Also, as more and more businesses make the transition to empowered teams, the organizations that cannot make the necessary changes may already be obsolete and not yet know that they are in serious trouble. For example, a small group of people shared with me that the company they worked for had made it to Style 4 Leadership – Empowered

Teams and they were extremely fulfilled working with people and leaders who respected them and got them involved in driving for excellence. This group decided to volunteer together to do some work for a non-profit organization that was still using old style management practices (use of fear, poor communications, silos, etc.). The experience was awful, especially when compared to what they experienced in their work environment. They shared with me that they will never consider volunteering for this organization again. This fairly large, well-known, non-profit institution may one day run out of volunteers and the executives may wonder what went wrong as they shut their doors.

There are four primary ways to get more productivity from your employees: 1) Fear; 2) Bribes and Incentives; 3) Improving the System; and 4) "Enthusiastic Productivity" (teamwork, process improvement, empowerment, trust, respect) that was mentioned in the previous chapter (Figure 10.1). Fear may work for a short time (you better do your job right or you will be fired!) but it causes the workers to want to resist and eventually fight back or shut down. Incentives and bribes (better pay, bonuses, or promotions) might work for a short time but can also have a negative impact to the rest of the organization (Why did she get a bonus and I didn't??? It is not fair!) and promotes individual accomplishments. Fear and incentives assume that most of the issues are being driven by a labor component instead of the process and overall system. This leads to the third way to increase productivity known as Continuous Improvement. However, many improvements are short-lived if employees are not fully

FIGURE 10.1
Types of Productivity Enhancements.

involved and they do not buy into the changes. Instead, *teams* of employees need to be rewarded and recognized for improvements made, problems that have been solved, and going beyond expectations in order to meet the needs of their customers. If this happens, the organization will experience what I like to call "Enthusiastic Productivity."

Enthusiastic productivity is achieved when an organization truly reaches Style 4 Leadership – Empowered Teams and everyone is working together to try and improve, innovate, and standardize their processes. Almost every employee I have spoken with that has worked in this type of environment has told me that they would never want to work in any other way and would do anything they could to make sure that the organization is successful, that their team is effective, and that their customers are happy. This can give that business or organization a significant competitive advantage. Also, keep in mind that as the processes improve and the teams deal with the day-to-day decisions, this frees up resources to focus on new products, new services, and other enhancements.

Of course, "enthusiastic productivity" is only a competitive advantage if several other aspects are in place. First, this assumes that the organization is providing a product or service that the customer wants. Next, the customer must value good quality, speed of delivery, and future product or service enhancements. And, the marketing team will need to communicate these improvements in a way that differentiates the organization from its competitors.

Achieving this level of enthusiasm does not happen overnight and requires all aspects of the system to work in concert with each other in a near flawless way. For example, let's assume that an organization has Style 4 leaders in every area except purchasing, which still has an old-style manager running things, and that manager buys shoddy materials in order to hit a personal objective of achieving the lowest price. The workers will quickly run into problems and realize that the efforts of achieving excellence are a façade. This is why it is critically important to have every leader in the organization on board with this new way of doing things, especially the top folks (Board of Directors, CEOs, owners, etc.).

Too many times, I have witnessed what I like to call the "10 percenters." These are organizations whose executives say they are doing improvements but end up barely scratching the surface. They might do a bit of cleaning and organizing but never make the deep commitment to fundamentally change how they manage, lead, and interact with each other and their workers. This creates a façade of excellence that fades quickly. A step up from the "10 percenters" are the "50 percenters." These organizations might have made it to Style 2 leadership or maybe even Style 3 with a few sporadic work teams with no plans to go any further. They are slightly engaging their employees by asking for their ideas, but never plan to change the culture, how they measure success, or empower anyone.

The 100 percenters have defined a new normal of leadership and culture that embraces their workers, continuously improves and drives innovation within their processes, and works tirelessly to meet and exceed the needs of their customers in order to achieve true excellence. They have completely overhauled their metric system and shifted individual goals and objectives to ones focused on the success of their teams. They have also redefined what a good leader is, how they act, and what they work on to help the teams achieve excellence. They reward, recognize, and promote leaders who have truly empowered their teams of employees. This sends a strong message that the old ways of managing using fear and control are being replaced with coaching, mentoring, supportive communication, vision setting, and enforcing organizational values such as teamwork, respect, and humbleness.

VALUES

Earlier in this book, we looked at Mission, Vision, and Strategy. Now it is time to include the fourth characteristic that is directly tied into Style 4 Leadership: Values (See Figure 6.1). What are the values needed to be successful with empowered teams? I posed this question on social media and in my workshops and got the following inputs (note: the order is based on an average of inputs after asking participants to rank the priority based on the values they would like to see in a collaborative organization):

- Customer Centric: Constantly Evaluating Feedback with Goal to Exceed Expectations
- Respect for Others: Compassion, Caring, Approachable
- Integrity and Honesty: Ethical, Candor
- Transparency and Openness: Humbleness, Thankfulness, Humor
- Trust and Sincerity: Credibility
- Positive Vision and Purpose: Inspirational, Exciting, Provides Focus, Longevity

- Continuous Improvement Mindset: Always Striving to Get Better, Building on Past Improvements, Not Being Satisfied with Anything Less than 100%
- Accountability: Priority Tasks Done in a Safe and Timely Manner, Responsibility
- Focus on Excellence: Competence and Effectiveness, Commitment, Passion
- Communication and Listening: Timely Data Sharing, Encouragement and Feedback
- Leadership: Empowerment, Inspirational, Motivational, Promotes Buy-In
- Diversity and Inclusion: Value All Inputs/Points of Views
- Continuous Learning and Development of Skills
- Building Effective Teams/Teamwork: Collaboration, Creativity, Appreciate All Members
- Standardization of Processes: Organization, Well-Documented Processes
- Optimism and Passion: Excitement, Encouragement, Inspirational
- Work/Life Balance: Fitness and Health, Promote Community Volunteer Service
- Persistence and Perseverance: Commitment, Courage, Patience
- Organizational Agility: Flexible, Dealing with Ambiguity
- Humility and Thankfulness: Harmony, Composure
- Sustainability: Goal of Zero Impact on the Environment, Reuse, Recycle
- Timely Decision Making: Open-Mindedness, Forward Thinking, Adaptability

Some additional values to consider that do not make the usual lists:

- Acceptance of Failure: A willingness to allow teams to try new ideas and as long as they follow specific guidelines, allowing them to fail, learn, and grow
- Encouraging Outlandish Ideas: Allowing team members to discuss multiple ideas before settling on a specific path; encourage creative, far-reaching, crazy ideas
- Reassurance that Sharing Bad News Is Good News: The only way to truly improve is to be willing to share problems that occur in the process

- Focus on Blaming the Process Not the People: Most people want to do a good job but become frustrated when they are forced to work in a bad process
- Striving to Reach Consensus When Practical: It takes a bit more time to get everyone on board with a particular decision but this investment is well worth the effort because it promotes ownership of the plan (note: "When Practical" refers to situations such as when in a crisis, a Style 1 leader may need to step in and make the decisions)

An interesting exercise is to take all of these different values (and others that might be specific to your organization or industry), write down each on a different index card, and share them with your organization's leadership team. Then, ask them to sort the cards from the most important value to the least important value. The way I usually facilitate this exercise is to spread the cards on a long table and then ask the leaders to move the cards around in silence until they reach agreement on the order of the cards (or they run out of time). We then discuss the order and try to reach consensus that these are the correct values to describe the future of the organization. Once the priority order is established, ask the leadership team to draw a line that separates the "critical" values from those that are just "important." The objective would be to have no more than 10 "critical" values. One way to determine which values are deemed to be critical is to ask the question, "If a candidate you were interviewing to join the organization clearly did not possess or even think a specific value was important or necessary, would you still hire this person?" If the answer is no, even if the candidate had a stellar résumé, then that value is considered to be "critical."

Once the "critical" values have been identified, the leaders need to determine if they are being demonstrated within the organization. What is the difference between a real value and one that is desired? A good exercise for the leadership team is to ask them to list concrete examples of where and how a particular value has been demonstrated within the organization. If this is difficult or impossible to do, then that value is not currently present in the culture of the organization. Next, talk to the employees to validate the leaders' perceptions. The leadership team will then want to discuss what needs to change in order to make the missing values more prominent. If the organization is unwilling to make the necessary changes, then that particular value needs to be removed from the list or the organization will eventually see it for what it truly is, a façade.

My experience is that individual workers have a difficult (but not impossible) path toward adopting a new set of values. It is essential to hire people who fit the critical values of the organization. When my team hired new employees, for example, I reminded the people who were participating in the interviewing process that it is far easier to teach someone a skill or something about a process than it is to change their views on how to treat other employees or their teammates. Our hiring process included a time at the end for all of the interviewers to come together to discuss each candidate. If even one team member, who was part of the interviewing process, said that they did not think a particular candidate possessed the values that the organization deemed to be "critical," we would turn down that candidate, even if they fit the role in all other ways. We eventually got to the point where we would list these "critical" values of the organization in the job descriptions in order to emphasize the direction that the company was heading. As part of the interview, we would ask the candidates to share with us concrete examples of ways that they might have demonstrated these values. If this proved to be difficult for the candidate, or the examples were contradicted, vague, or flimsy, the usual consensus of the team would be to find someone else.

Defining and demonstrating values at all levels of the organization are a critical component to achieving Style 4 – Empowerment Leadership. The leaders need to set the example for how they expect employees to work together in order to achieve truly empowered teams. This can get messy if the employees are told to use one set of defined values and then see their leaders behaving in an entirely different manner. The confusion that this will create will almost guarantee that the teams will eventually fail. For example, if the leaders say that trust, respect, and teamwork are critical values but, at the same time, they are still using fear, intimidation, and individual rewards and recognition, the employees will either shut the team down by refusing to participate or they will begin to mimic their leaders, which will eventually splinter and destroy the teams.

The organizational leaders need to take a critical look at all aspects of their behavior and not gloss over or rationalize anything that contradicts a specific value. For example, in one organization, they ranked "respect for others" as a critical value. The leadership team struggled to understand why their employees would shake their heads and chuckle whenever they wanted to discuss this particular value. They asked me to help them figure out where the disconnect between their words and reality was occurring. I sat in on one of their leadership team meetings and the problem became apparent fairly quickly. The leadership team enjoyed "slamming" each other. Slamming is a disruptive behavior in a team where someone makes a joke at someone else's expense, usually someone in the room (note that it is encouraged to have some lighthearted fun within a team in order to build comradery, just not at the expense of someone else). The way this plays out is that one leader would say something like, "Hey Joe, I saw you on the golf course the other day and you were hitting more balls into the lake than on the green. Ha. Ha." Slams usually start off small and innocent. Of course, Joe, in order to save face, must eventually slam back. "Hey Steve, I saw you driving down the road the other day in your new car and I was worried that it was going to fall apart before you got home. I hope you did not pay much money for that piece of junk. Ha. Ha." Each slam escalates in intensity. "Joe, you know, the other day, I walked through your department and your employees looked bewildered and confused. Maybe you could buy them a *Manufacturing for Dummies* book. Ha. Ha." Now the slams become personal and start dragging others into the mix. These escalations continue until someone shouts something like "Your mama is so..." In other words, things can get nasty fairly quickly.

After observing this behavior, I asked the employees what they thought of their leadership team. They told me that, clearly, their leaders absolutely and completely hated and despised each other. When I shared this back to the leadership team, they were stunned and immediately became defensive. "Are you saying we can't have a little fun and joke around?" "Sure," I explained. "You can joke all you want. Just don't make jokes that put each other down or impact anyone else in the organization." They decided to implement a "slam" jar and each agreed to pay $10 if they slammed someone else. The jar quickly began to fill with $10 bills (some were even prepaying and putting $20 bills in the jar). At the end of the meeting, they emptied out the jar and had over $500 accumulated (which they donated to a local charity). This was a huge wakeup call and they put a sign up in their meeting room that stated "No Slamming Allowed!" I returned several months later and the atmosphere had changed significantly throughout the entire organization. The value listed as "respect for others" was now being demonstrated at all levels and had become a reality throughout the organization.

For those organizations that still plan to use Management by Objectives (see Chapter 3), one way to move closer to utilizing this new definition of leadership would be to add an assessment component that emphasizes values. Each employee would be evaluated on how many of the goals and objectives were met as well as how well they demonstrated the values that are critical to the organization. Since this last part is subjective, the boss may need to get input from several sources to accurately make this assessment. The boss would then use the following 9-block diagram and put an "X" in the block that best describes the employee (Figure 10.2).

If the X is placed in the High Values Demonstrated/High Objectives Met block (A), then this would represent a "superstar" in the organization who needs to be coached and mentored for greater opportunities. The average employee is in the middle block (B). Every organization will have many good, solid workers who meet all expectations but have no desire to move into new, higher demanding roles. The Low/Low employee (C) may be in the wrong job, may have a broken process they are dealing with, or they may not understand the values. If none of these are true, then this person may not be a good fit for the organization. The tricky boxes are D and E. Block D (High Values Demonstrated/Low Objectives Met) could indicate a diamond in the rough. This employee may move to box A if they are able to find a job that is more fitting to their passions, skills, and gifts. Or, they may be in a broken process and, with a focus on continuous improvement, may begin to migrate to the right side of the 9-block as their process gets better. Block E represents an employee who gets the job done but does not meet the values that are critical to the organization. This person will need a great deal of coaching in order to move up the 9-block chart. However, rarely have I witnessed someone who can change the way they treat others. It is possible, but the company leaders will need to be prepared to replace

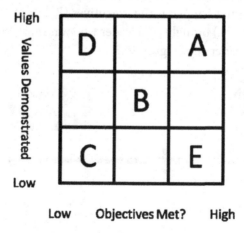

FIGURE 10.2
Utilizing 9-Block for Employee Evaluations.

this person, if needed, in order to elevate the rest of the team. Many times, when this happens, it is like a dark cloud has been lifted and the rest of the organization begins to thrive.

Eventually, the organization would want to replace the "Objectives Met?" with "Team Goals and Objectives Met?" This would help the organization move closer to Style 4 – Empowered Team status. The definition of an outstanding employee would then be someone who demonstrates all of the critical values, plays a significant role on the team (as a leader, facilitator, and/or as a contributor who supports others on the team), and is part of a team that exceeds all of their expectations.

MATCHING LEADERS WITH THE CURRENT MATURITY OF THE ORGANIZATION

The best leaders are those who can flex from Style 1 to Style 4 depending on the current needs of the organization. However, some leaders are more comfortable with a specific style and will want to use that way to lead as much as possible (even if that means trying to move the organization to that place on the progression chart). This can have a devastating impact on the successful growth of the teams, the employees, and the overall organization. For example, imagine an organization that has grown and progressed through Style 1 (Crisis Leader), Style 2 (Idea Gathering Leader), Style 3 (Team Forming Leader), and is ready for Style 4 (Empowerment Leader). What would happen if the executives (Board of Directors, CEO, owner, President, etc.) brought on a leader who was most comfortable with Style 1 – Crisis Leadership (Figure 10.3)?

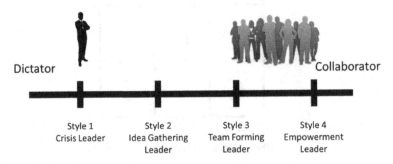

FIGURE 10.3
Mismatch of Leadership Style and Needs.

The first thing that this new leader would probably do is to identify or even create some sort of crisis within the organization. They would then begin to dictate orders to the employees as if the crisis were real. The teams of employees might be able to accommodate this new leader for a short period of time, hoping that when the crisis ended, they could go back to the collaboration side of the Progression Model. However, since the leader is most comfortable in Style 1, they will constantly look for new crises in order to keep playing the dictator role. The organization will eventually get frustrated and either slide back to Style 1 and accept that it no longer needs to think, make decisions, or participate in improvement efforts, or the employees will rebel and try to move the leader over to the collaboration side of the Progression Model or get the leader replaced. Either outcome will do great damage to the organization or, at a minimum, delay the progressive growth toward empowered teams.

The opposite scenario can be just as devastating to the organization. Imagine what would happen if the organization was accustomed to a Style 1 – Crisis Leader (who may have kept the organization at Style 1 for too long), and then the executives hired a Style 4 – Empowerment Leader (Figure 10.4).

I have seen this happen when an organization tries to accelerate the progress toward achieving empowered teams, not realizing the damage that will occur. As has been discussed throughout this book, there are many elements that must be in place in order to achieve Style 4. The Mission, Vision, Strategy, and Values all need to be defined, adopted, and demonstrated on a consistent basis. All of the employees will need to go through multiple rounds of training in order to expose them to the improvement tools and methodologies as well as teach them how to work together as a team. And, the organization will need to develop its

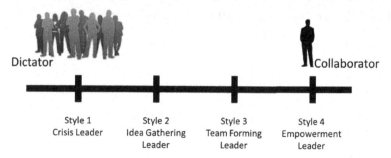

FIGURE 10.4
Mismatch of Leadership Style and Needs.

critical thinking skills (Style 2) as well as experience what it is like to work together to solve isolated problems (Style 3). If the employees are thrown into teams and told they must start making critical day-to-day decisions without this foundation, there is a high probability that they will flounder, fail, and possibly even shut down. Eventually, the Style 4 leader will get frustrated with the lack of progress and will more than likely resign and try to find a company that has made further progress.

For these reasons, it is important for Human Resources and the organization's executives to understand the following:

1) The differences between the four styles of leadership
2) A map of where each part of the organization is on the Leadership Progression Model
3) An understanding of what is needed to move each part of the organization to the next leadership style (such as more training, experience, working on more difficult problems, etc.)
4) A clear definition of the organization's Mission, an inspirational Vision of where the company is going over the next few years, a Strategy that has a defined list of action items to make the vision a reality, and a well-thought-out set of Values that are demonstrated on a regular basis
5) And most importantly, when filling a new leadership position within the organization, finding one who is compatible with the current organization's position on the Leadership Progression Model and who will also help move the organization to the next level

When these steps are followed, there is a greater chance that progress will continue toward collaboration even when a new leader comes on board. This is critically important in order to assure continued growth toward collaboration and achieving "enthusiastic productivity."

11

Defining a New Normal of Leadership...

What exactly is the definition of excellence?

THE STORY OF MARY ROBINSON, PRODUCTION WORKER FOR JED, INC.

Tick... Tick... Tick

Mary kept staring at the clock. She was only two hours into her shift but it felt like she had been sitting here, staring at the clock, for days. She literally had nothing to do but breathe. Time slowed and she started to watch a cockroach crawl down the wall. "Finally, something to do," she thought as the bug made its way closer to the floor. "Maybe I can think of a name for it to challenge my mind and pass the time."

Mary had nothing to do because her production line was not producing anything. Her overbearing supervisor told her to sit at her workstation so she would be ready to go when the line started producing again. Of course, he had no idea when that might be.

As Mary fought hard to keep from zoning out, she faintly heard the voice of her cruel, spiteful supervisor yell at one of her former team members. "What do you mean you can't put part 'A' and 'B' together?!? You are holding up the entire production line!!! My employee utilization numbers are going down the drain because of you!!!"

"These parts we got from that new supplier suck," replied the worker. "There is no way they meet the engineering specifications. You try to put them together!"

"Did a quality inspector check them? Do you have the engineering drawings?" asked the supervisor.

"The quality folks are working on a multitude of fires and cannot spare anyone. I tried calling engineering but apparently, their new manager moved them all to an off-site location and told them to only focus on developing new products since that was his new objective. When I tried calling the engineer who was assigned to this area in the past, he told me that he was sorry but to save his job he had to quit talking to me... and then he hung up the phone."

"Well, we have got to get this line back up and running... I don't care what it takes. Grab a freaking hammer and bang the parts together! Force them to fit so we can get something out the door today. Do I make myself clear?!?"

As Mary listened to this exchange, a wave of emotions hit her like a sledgehammer. First, she felt pity for her former teammate and for the supervisor. This quickly turned to resentment and a scowl began to form on her face. Then, she realized there was absolutely nothing she could do and a feeling of apathy and defeat swept over her. She let out a long sigh. "I can't take this much longer," she thought.

"Mary! Get back to work!" shouted her supervisor.

"I don't have anything to work on," replied Mary. Her supervisor walked over and looked at her empty workstation.

"Well, at least look like you are busy. I don't want the new vice president..."

"You mean Frank Smith, Jr.?" interrupted Mary.

"You workers better stop calling him that if you know what is good for you," said Mary's supervisor. "Well, I don't want Frank Jr. to ream me out for having a lazy, do-nothing employee being paid to just sit around."

Something snapped deep down inside Mary. Her boss was right. She could no longer sit here and do nothing. She stood up, grabbed her coat, purse, and lunch bag and began walking toward the exit. "Where do you think you are going?" said her supervisor. "Mary, get back here this instant! I swear I will have you fired if you walk out that exit!!!"

The next few hours were a bit of a blur. Mary got into her car, looked up the JED, Inc. corporate headquarters address, plugged this information into her phone's GPS, and began driving. The next thing Mary knew, she was standing outside a tall building in the middle of a city she rarely visited. Fortunately, her company badge was the same style as everyone else's and the security guard allowed her to enter into the main lobby area. She found a bank of elevators and stepped inside one that had just opened.

"Dang, it looks like a special key is required to get to the floor I want," she thought. Fortune was on her side this day. An employee stepped in just as the doors were closing and put his key into the panel and pushed the button for the top floor. "That is where I am going too," Mary said. The employee did not say anything and did not seem to care where Mary went.

The elevator doors opened on the top floor and Mary stepped into a plush lobby. Expensive artwork covered the walls, the chairs were all overstuffed and comfortable looking, and the desks were made out of luxurious, polished wood. The pleasant smell of cappuccinos and pastries whiffed through the air. Again, fortune was with Mary as she noticed that the receptionist was away from her desk. There was a hallway behind this desk with thick carpeting and wood paneling covering the walls. "This must be the right direction," thought Mary. In order to better blend in, she picked up a binder that was sitting on one of the tables and began strolling down the hallway. After walking for what seemed like hours (only a couple of minutes in reality), she noticed a large conference room that had several people inside. Through the window in the door, she could see sitting at the head of a long boardroom type table, the person she wanted to talk with... the CEO of JED, Inc. Mary gathered up every ounce of courage, pushed opened the door, and fell flat on her face as her shoe caught on the door jam.

Whoever was speaking immediately stopped and everyone turned to look at this new person who invaded their meeting. "Are you alright?" asked the CEO. A couple of people near the door helped Mary get back on her feet. Fortunately, the plush carpeting absorbed most of the impact of the fall. "Yes, no broken bones, just a broken ego," said Mary.

"That is good. I don't think you are in the right place," said the CEO. "Let me call my assistant and he can help you."

"No. This is the right place," replied Mary. "I have driven several hours to talk to you. I am one of your employees at the business Jim Brown led up until a month ago."

"Do you want me to call security?" asked one of the attendees.

"No, everything is under control," said the CEO. He had already pushed the panic button that was located under the long table and knew that security were on their way. "What did you want to tell me Ms....?"

"Mary, Mary Robinson. It is really more of a question. Why? Why did you promote Frank Smith and fire Jim Brown?"

"Well, I did not fire Jim. I guess he and Frank did not see eye to eye and Frank was the one who removed him from office."

"Jim was the best leader we have ever had in this company. Our productivity numbers and key performance metrics were setting records. In fact, just a month ago, the day before Jim was escorted out of the building, we achieved 100% in all of our metrics for the day. Now, the production lines barely run, our quality numbers are awful, and we are missing most of our ship dates. I don't understand. How could you let this happen?"

"Calm down Ms. Robinson. I can see you have real passion over this concern. The new president of your division, Frank Smith, has made it clear that those past numbers were all fabricated. Jim clearly lied to you, to us, and to himself in order to do anything he could to get promoted. You and the rest of the workers should be relieved. I heard that he forced the workers to actually make day-to-day decisions and to think of ways to make things work smoother. Now that burden is gone, you no longer need to think or be responsible for any decisions."

"What?!?" exclaimed Mary as she shook her head in disbelief. "None of that is true. Jim had real respect for all of the employees and gave us the training and tools required to achieve excellence. He greeted each of us as we walked in and routinely asked how he could help. When he discovered that the quality metrics were wrong, he gathered all of the employees together and told us to be honest when reporting failures. To drive this point home, he tore a stack of data sheets and threw them into the trash."

"Well, there were other considerations," said the CEO. "We got letters from customers who complained that their orders were not shipped on time."

Mary thought for a moment and then said, "Oh, you must be referring to the time we worked extra hard to get an emergency order out for our largest customer. Yeah, a few orders slipped, but Jim Brown called every one of those customers, told them about the warehouse fire, and got permission to change the ship dates. Wayne Green, the president of our largest customer was so thankful, he and his employees chipped in to buy Jim and his wife a large teddy bear for their new daughter. Over the past 6 months, we have received dozens and dozens of letters from customers who were thrilled with our quality and delivery performance.

"Hmmm..." thought the CEO out loud. "Maybe I need to look into this and rethink my decision. This is a brave thing you are doing coming here to share your point of view with me."

Mary began to relax a bit and thought that she was having a real impact. The CEO noticed someone new had entered the conference room. "Ah, here are the security guards. Please escort Ms. Robinson out of the building and make sure she is not allowed to return. I plan to let Frank know about this intrusion so he can make sure that this insubordination is dealt with!"

As soon as one of the guards placed his hand on Mary's shoulder, she blinked and found herself back at her workstation staring at the cockroach. She then realized that it was all just a figment of her imagination and that neither she nor anyone else in the company had the courage to confront their CEO.

"Mary, I thought I told you to get back to work!" said her supervisor. "Look busy or I will be forced to write you up and send you home."

Buzzzzz.... Buzzzzz...

Mary's phone lit up indicating that she had a text message. She glanced down and read what the message said on the screen. Her entire spirit transformed like a butterfly breaking out of its cocoon and for the first time in weeks, Mary smiled. The message read:

Mary, call me tonight. I have an open job in my new company with your name on it. J. Brown.

THE STORY OF JIM BROWN – 5 WEEKS PRIOR

"I tried to stop them," said Officer Joe. "But they insisted on seeing you escorted out of the building." Jim Brown was packing all of his personal possessions into a large, cardboard box. The past 24 hours consisted of a huge range of emotions; from achieving 100% performance metrics to finding out that his operations leader was leaving to being fired to now packing up his office late at night. Frank Smith had made it clear that he wasn't allowed to talk to anyone or tell his employees, his extended family really, good-bye.

"It's okay Joe," replied Jim with a heavy voice.

"Well, I am not going to stand for this!" said Joe. "You were the best leader we have ever had and they are treating you like some sort of criminal. I refuse to go along with this travesty!"

An hour later, Joe and Jim were standing together in the employee parking lot, each with their own box of personal items.

"Thank you for your loyalty, Joe. I hate that you got swept up in all of this. I will give Frank Smith a call tomorrow and try and get you your job back."

"No... thank you for the offer but I will be alright. Something tells me that this might be for the best. If you ever need a security guard, keep me in mind."

"I will do that," replied Jim. "In their haste to get me out of here, they did not have me sign any sort of non-compete document. I am free to contact and talk to anyone I want to hire from JED, Inc. anytime I want. I think they might regret making that mistake." With that said, Jim shook Joe's hand and he headed home.

A few days later, Susan Jones, Jim's old operations leader, called. "Hey Jim, it sounds like I left JED, Inc. just in the nick of time. How is unemployment treating you?"

"Well, it has given me a lot more time to spend with my wife and daughter. I am starting to get the hang of being a stay-at-home dad."

"That sounds nice. So, I guess you would not be interested in interviewing for a divisional president's job in my new company? My boss just announced he was taking a corporate role and wanted to know if you might be interested in his old position."

"I don't know Susan," replied Jim. "Thank you for the consideration but I got burned so badly in my last assignment. It has taught me to be extra careful before jumping into anything new."

"Do you remember that diagram you shared with us in one of our staff meetings that showed the four different styles of leaders?" asked Susan. "In the short time I have spent in this new role, it is easy to see that the CEO and all of the executives would qualify for the collaborative, style four side of the progression. They have made it clear that they want to go down the exact same path you took us through in order to get to empowered teams. So far, everything I have experienced indicates that they are sincere. And the business is not that far from your current home, so you and your family would be able to stay in town."

"That does sound intriguing," said Jim. "Danielle, my wife, has a new job at the hospital. We are committed to this location for a few more years. Alright, set up the interview. Oh, and do you know if they need a good security guard? I happen to know someone who would do an outstanding job."

A few days later, Jim was sitting in the office of the CEO of Susan's employer, signing all of the paperwork making him Susan's boss once again. Soon after, a group of corporate leaders, which included Jim and Susan, developed a 3-year vision and strategy that would transform the company in order to compete well into the next decade and beyond. Several open leadership positions were filled with JED, Inc. cast-offs.

A few weeks later, Susan went to see Jim with a request. "I know we are months away from being ready to form our first employee problem-solving team," said Susan. "However, don't you think it would be a good idea to hire someone who has demonstrated the ability to work with a variety of people and has good ideas on ways to improve?"

Jim began to laugh. "I am one step ahead of you. I just sent Mary Robinson a text to call me tonight. She would be a terrific person to help model the way for our entire workforce."

THE STORY OF FRANK SMITH

"What do you mean you are not pleased with how things are going?" Frank Smith had now been the Divisional President for a little over a year. He had done a thorough job of wiping out all of the leaders and teams and replacing them with 'old-style' managers. However, even with all of Frank's tricks that he used to manipulate the performance metrics, it was clear that customer complaints had skyrocketed, sales were dropping, and JED, Inc. was starting to see a lot of red ink on the financial reports.

"According to the data, we are in a free fall," said the CEO. "Recently, I met with your two vice presidents and they lifted up some rather significant issues about your management style. They shared with me that you have tied their hands and they are not allowed to run their businesses or make any decisions without your direct approval." Frank's face turned bright red as he realized that his top two employees had stabbed him in the back and thrown him under a bus.

"Those two idiots don't know how to run a business like I do," replied Frank. "It is important that I am part of the decision-making process in order to make sure everything stays on track and we are able to achieve my objectives for this division."

"Apparently, your inaccessibility has resulted in a significant crisis in the decision-making process. Look Frank, you were a good, solid manager when it came to running one small business. However, it is clear to me that you are in way over your head when it comes to running multiple plants and managing multiple staffs. Unfortunately, the Board of Directors and I have reached the conclusion that you are no longer a good fit for this position or for this company. Don't worry. We are prepared to give you a generous severance package as long as you sign several legal documents that will prevent you from doing any additional harm to this company."

Later that day, after Frank was escorted out of the building, the CEO sat down with the Corporate President of Human Resources. "We need to fill Frank's old job quickly so we can right this ship before it sinks. Let's bring in that vice president we hired a year ago to take Jim Brown's old job. He seems like a solid manager."

The HR executive wrote on his notepad; "Boss wants me to bring in the guy who they hired to replace Jim Brown. I think the workers gave him the nickname Frank Smith, Jr. I wonder if we are about to make the same mistake?"

And the cycle of using "old-style" managers remained unbroken at JED, Inc.

THE STORY OF JIM BROWN

The large ballroom erupted in thunderous applause as Jim Brown made his way up to the podium. It had been 2 and a half years since Jim was let go from JED, Inc. and accepted his current position. The large audience of people from all sorts of different industries and organizations included Jim's wife, Danielle, who was beginning to show evidence of their second child, Jim's leadership team and boss (the CEO of his current company), and several employees.

"I am grateful to this association to be the recipient of this honor recognizing the outstanding performance of our business," said Jim. "However, I am not the one who should be receiving this award. I would like to ask the employees who are here to join me at this podium." Several people stood up and began to walk up to the front of the large ballroom. This group included production workers, maintenance personnel, team leaders, engineers, and customer service call takers. Over a dozen people snaked their way between the large round tables that filled the floor of the ballroom. The rest of the crowd began to applaud this group of workers and as they reached the podium, Jim's staff and the company CEO led the audience to their feet in order to give them a standing ovation.

Mary Robinson walked up to the microphone at the podium and spoke in a nervous voice. "I think that all of the company leaders need to join us up here as well. We would not have been able to explore the possibility of forming employee empowered teams that eventually led to this celebration of excellence if it had not been for their guidance, coaching, vision, and leadership!" The room once again applauded as the rest of the group made their way to the front of the room. "This award is truly an honor," Mary continued. "However, many of you might not know that last month our company was honored in a slightly different way. Our state government did a survey and we got the highest marks from our entire workforce which gave us the honor of being recognized as a Best Place to Work!"

With that said, the entire ballroom erupted in applause once again and all of the employees, executives, team leaders, and workers were all beaming with huge smiles. Jim Brown looked at the group of employees standing with him, and realized that there was so much more to life than being seen as the one in total control, using fear to drive for better results... in other words the old way of managing people. He leaned over to Mary and said just loud enough for her to hear, "Working with great people on a winning team, who are all pulling together to achieve a common vision, that is my new definition of achieving excellence."

PRACTICAL APPLICATIONS

Several times, throughout my career, I dreamed the same dream that Mary had in the story portion of this chapter. One bad manager seemed to be replaced by another bad manager and I would think to myself, "Why does this keep happening? Can't the leaders see the damage that is being done by promoting 'old style' managers? Somebody needs to talk some sense into our company executives." Remember, we are trying to overcome decades and decades of a certain definition that is used to recognize and promote people into executive positions. The real question is; "How do we break the chain?"

We need to define a new normal of leadership. What are the characteristics of a person who will have the best chance of leading an organization to excellence?

1) *A leader who can flex between all four Leadership Styles* – This person understands all of the different ways to lead, can assess a given situation and select the appropriate leadership style, and feels comfortable switching from style to style depending on the current

needs of the organization with the goal of eventually migrating the entire organization to Style 4 Leadership – Empowered Teams.

2) *Develops trust and respect with all of the employees* – A good leader knows how to build relationships with people who hold any and all jobs within the organization. They communicate in a way that helps the employees understand the future vision, the current situation, and what is required to achieve success. If something goes wrong, the focus is on fixing the process, not blaming the people.

3) *Creates a culture that embraces change and is not satisfied with settling for "good enough"* – It is easy to become complacent, especially when things are going fairly well. A good leader continuously pushes the organization toward figuring out a way to improve, even if it means breaking a good process in order to make it better. This requires the removal of fear to try new things and the need to consistently utilize Plan, Do, Check (or Study), Act and the recognition that ideas that do not give the expected results should be celebrated as a step toward coming up with an idea that will eventually make the process better.

4) *Lifts up the teams of employees while also steering the ship* – The responsibility of the overall direction, performance, and success still rides on the shoulders of the leader. However, a leader of empowered teams of employees needs to possess a great deal of humility and understand that while he or she might be steering the ship, the employees are the ones who are providing power to the propellers. Each is worthless without the other. Whenever something good happens (customers provide positive feedback, achieving milestone metrics, receiving an award), the entire organization needs to share in the glory of the moment. On the other hand, a good leader will absorb any arrows representing bad news and protect their teams.

5) *Knows how to hire good people and helps to develop their talents* – Since the vision is to one day get the entire organization to empowered teams, the new normal of leadership includes the understanding of the importance of hiring people who fit the values of the organization. This requires a well thought out process to find, interview, and assess each candidate and a willingness to take a pass on questionable people in order to find the right fit, even if this prolongs the hiring process. The goal is to hire people with the right technical (competencies) foundation, the appropriate interpersonal (team) skills, and has all of the values the organization has defined as being critical to their future success. Everything else can be taught. Once people are on

the payroll, the leader understands the importance of developing and enhancing the skills of the employee through regular training opportunities, by exposing them to new ideas (benchmarking other organizations, for example), and by giving them new assignments to grow their list of talents.

6) *Sticks with the vision and strategy even when problems occur* – It is easy to give up and go back to the comfort zone of decades of bad management practices when there are bumps in the road. A good leader will push through roadblocks and use them as learning opportunities to help their employees and teams grow and mature. This may require the leader to stand up to their Board of Directors, owner, CEO, etc. and not back down in order to permanently transform the organization. This transformation may take years, so the leader must be ready to play the long game and educate, communicate, and "lead up" to win over the upper echelon of the organization.

7) *Puts ego aside and carries on with a vision that a predecessor began* – There is a perception (or is it a reality?) that a new leader must destroy everything their predecessor began and start over in order to get credit for future improvements. Since transforming the culture may take years to accomplish, this is something that must change. One organization was well on their way to Style 4 leadership, for example, with several fully empowered teams about to be launched. The leader got promoted and the executives brought on a new person who they thought would carry on with the original vision. However, the new leader took the business back to Style 1 – Crisis Leadership and began the entire process over in order to put his own spin on things. This included coming up with a new vision and strategy and they even reprioritized the values. Two years of progress were erased, along with a great deal of trust between the employees and the leader.

8) *Understands that it is all about pleasing the customer* – If the organization does not provide a good product or service in a timely manner at a cost that is competitive, the rest of this book is irrelevant. Everything that is done, improving processes, building trust, developing teams, solving problems, must keep the customer as the main focus. I am a big fan of setting up employee, customer visits. This does two things. First, the employees get a chance to connect real people's faces to the product and/or service that they are providing. This will enhance the "enthusiastic productivity"

that can help drive better outcomes and give the organization a competitive advantage. Second, if the organization has truly made it to Style 4 collaborative leadership, the customer will be blown away by the focus on excellence. Over the years, I have had several customers tell me that the production facility, robust processes, and the employee teams were our greatest selling feature and were among their top considerations when buying from our company. Again, it is impossible to connect a revenue or profit amount to something that is significantly intangible. However, there is no doubt of the positive impact.

THE DAY IN THE LIFE OF A STYLE 4 LEADER

In this new normal of leadership, what might a typical day look like for the organization's leader? The Style 4 leader might want to greet employees as they arrive for the day and then sit in on one of the empowered team's shift start-up meetings. Next, the leader might want to spend time with a customer to better understand how the organization is doing in meeting their expectations, what they could do better, and discuss future trends and needs. After this, the leader might sit down with one of the members of their leadership team to provide coaching and mentoring, listen to what is going well within the organization and what could be better, and discuss ways to improve the culture and help the teams succeed. Once this is complete, the leader may then sit in on a report out from one of the improvement teams and then spend some time walking the process and talking to employees to try and better understand what is working well and what can be improved. This might include sitting down with a group of employees at lunch in order to build better relationships. The leader then might want to sit in on a meeting between purchasing and a supplier in order to discuss ways they can work together better and improve the way they communicate. This could include future trends in demand so the supplier can be better prepared for any fluctuations that might impact their ability to supply good-quality products. The day might then wrap up with a huddle meeting with the entire leadership team to continue to discuss their vision, strategy, and values.

Notice what the leader is not doing. They are not fighting fires or focusing on ways to place the blame on someone if something goes wrong. They are not hiding in their office. They are not making all of the decisions, but they are plugged in and making sure that all areas of the organization are heading in a direction that supports the mission and vision. They are not acting like they are any more important or above anyone else in the organization even though they do carry the weight of making sure the organization is successful.

BREAKING THE CHAIN

What will it take to break the chain of utilizing 'old style' management techniques? There are several ways this might happen and they fall into two camps: Reactive and Proactive.

Reactively breaking the chain – If a competitor begins to migrate toward collaborative, empowered teams, then every other business in that industry is in trouble and better hope they fail. By the time it becomes evident that this competitor is making progress (stealing market share, lower prices, better customer ratings, etc.), they have probably already moved to Style 3 leadership. This would put them 6 months to 2 years ahead of any other business that is just getting started which will make it difficult to catch up. Also, since most people want to enjoy their work and be part of a winning team, this competitor will be able to hire the best people, even stealing those from other companies in their industry.

At some point, we will reach a tipping point where a majority of businesses and organizations will have made progress toward this new normal of leadership. When this happens, any company, business, or organization that has not yet adopted this approach, will either scramble to break the chain of 'old style' managers in order to get on the right path or face eventual bankruptcy and collapse, plus no one will want to work there. Also, at some point, the most viable candidates for future leadership positions will only want to be a part of an organization that is respectful to all employees, focuses on improving processes utilizing teams, and is full of exciting people working together to achieve an electrifying, inspirational vision.

Proactively breaking the chain – It is always better to be in the lead position. However, getting all of the organization's leaders on board can be a daunting task. A strong CEO, with the backing of the Board of Directors, can make this happen fairly quickly. However, if the CEO (or top person in the organization) is on the fence, one of the people (a V.P. for example) at the next level might step up and take the lead. This will only be sustainable if this V.P. can eventually get the CEO to see the light and get most, if not all, of the other V.P.s on board. This means that there will be a double burden on the shoulders of this leader; changing the culture within their division of the organization and "leading up" in order to convince their peers and boss that this is the best path to follow. How can this V.P. win over the rest of the organization's leaders?

First, invite the executives to attend training classes, team report outs, and celebrations. There is a good chance that the V.P.'s peers won't attend (unless the boss also shows up), but the constant invitations might wear them down and will at least let them know that changes are in progress. Second, communicate any and all improvements throughout the organization. Some of these improvements might be applicable to other parts of the company and the V.P.'s peers can implement these ideas for free. Third, share metrics that will be relatable to the other leaders. Be sure to communicate the metrics at the beginning in order to set a baseline. The V.P. will need to make sure these metrics are accurate (like Jim Brown did in the story), even if this means starting over and collecting a few months of data that is more reflective of what is actually happening. After several successes occur (and there will be many, many successes if this is done correctly), there will be plenty of evidence to win over the leadership team. Unfortunately, if this does not happen, the V.P. who is leading the effort will become frustrated and he or she will eventually give up and leave. This could sign the death warrant of the organization.

Once the CEO is won over, keep in mind that the tenure of the main leader of the organization might only be a few months to a few years. During this time, it is critically important to move the ball far enough that it would become difficult to go back to the old ways of doing things. Also, the Board of Directors will need to know the type of leader to look for when eventually replacing the CEO. The good news is that as more and more organizations move down this path, the pool of Style 4 leaders will grow and the number of "old-style" managers will begin to shrink.

In order to change the culture of the business or organization, several steps need to take place. First, word needs to spread about the benefits and step function improvement in customer satisfaction associated with Style 4 leadership. Next, more future bosses will need to be exposed to and educated on different leadership styles. This may require business schools and universities to rethink and redesign their curriculum. And then, future Board of Director members and Human Resource professionals will need to begin working this new normal of leadership into their hiring process. Once these things have happened, the quality of work life will improve for all employees.

CONCLUSION

I have had the pleasure of working with several organizations over the years and help them achieve significant improvement and culture change. It is extremely satisfying to see a group of employees go from "*The Walking Dead*" to an enthusiastic, winning team. Again, this does not happen overnight and requires a great deal of dedicated effort at all levels. However, the payoff is tremendous and the leaders who participate in helping this transition will leave a legacy that will be long remembered after they have moved on or retired. Every employee, including the leaders, will eventually be required to leave their comfort zone of decades of bad management practices in order to make Style 4 leadership a reality. If the leaders are not fully committed to making this happen, a fake, flimsy façade will be created that will eventually crumble. When this happens, the employees will become frustrated, angry, tired, and hopeless... shells of their former selves.

The good news is that there are several examples of companies, organizations, hospitals, government groups, nonprofits, and service providers that have made significant progress down this path. Most of this is not rocket science. Anyone can put the principles spelled out in this book into place. It just takes a desire and a willingness to get started and then strong fortitude to see things through. There will be setbacks, bumps in the road, blockers to change, false starts, and unforeseen failures. Each of these will become learning opportunities that will make the organization stronger. And if done correctly, excellence will be achieved: Excellence in the metrics, excellence in customer satisfaction, excellence in the financials, and excellence in relationships between the leaders, peers, and employees.

When we retire and look back on our body of work, my hope is that one day, every organization will be voted by their employees a "Best Place to Work." As more and more *Jim Browns* are created and fewer *Frank Smiths* are promoted, this vision will one day become a reality.

Index

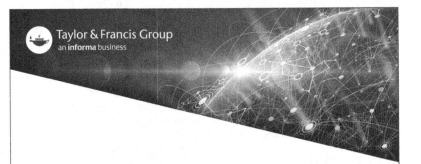